PRAISE FOR *WARRIOR UPGRADE*

"Honest, perceptive and full of useful, practical advice about how to lead a better life in the way of the (peaceful) warrior."
Mark Dapin – Award winning Writer and Journalist

"This is a story about one man, and yet it is a story about everyone; for those who feel incomplete, for those who can never achieve enough to gain their own self-approval, and for those for whom life always seems like a perpetual barrage of new and greater struggles.

In telling his story Andy offers us a mirror. And though his triumphs are uniquely his, and his pain and despair belong to him alone, it was my self-reflection at every page-turn that I found most powerful.

Warrior Upgrade *tells of re-discovering the self that was never lost, and it is a beautiful offering of gratitude, reminding us throughout that we are only here on account of the people that love us."*
Ed White – Champion athlete, Personal trainer, Corporate consultant, Life-long friend and student

"A thoughtful and insightful read, written with honesty and candour. From the perspective of a warrior and philosopher, there are many truths and observations in this book that all of us could use."
MayLai Paulin – Mother, Scientist, Long-time friend

"A fascinating story of how the struggles of youth can mould a person into a stronger and more resilient adult. Great lessons to be learnt by all. And above all of that, one of life's greatest challenges – Parkinson's Disease, which I am sure will be met with the same incredible determination."

Rob Ruffle – Fellow Parkinson's Fighter

"Whilst Andrew shows all the outer courage, determination, superb skills and fighting spirit on the mat and in the Dojo, is highly adept in the classical Japanese martial arts and his eclectic style of North Star Martial Arts, this is but a simulacrum of the inner work he has done that lies in the narrative of this book, Warrior Upgrade.

He has kept his own counsel on his battle with anxiety and the now mindfully-focused war he wages with Parkinson's Disease; this is the true test where his warriorship of calm abiding shines forth. Andrew's ability to walk his talk is so evident today, of moving states of mind into traits of embodiment. He is actualising the lessons and wisdom he shares in this book. Andrew's courage to write this book from a complete state of vulnerability and humility along with highly pragmatic steps of how we as individuals can cultivate higher pro social and pro emotional ways of being in the world, is commendable.

By writing and sharing his story Andrew Dickinson is a true Sensei in the literal Japanese meaning: A spirit or star who has been before showing the way with humility and grace."

Scott A Brown – 6th Dan, Shorinjiryu Kenkokan Karatedo

WARRIOR UPGRADE

Twenty Ways to Upgrade to a Warrior Life

ANDY DICKINSON

Copyright © 2023 Andrew Dickinson
Published by Andrew Dickinson
www.andydickinson.com.au
www.northstarmartialarts.com.au

The moral right of the author has been asserted.
For quantity sales or media enquiries, please contact the publisher at the website address above.

ISBN: 978-0-6484350-4-4 (paperback)
       978-0-6484350-5-1 (ebook)

Proofreading by Bill Harper
Cover Photograph by Shane Carn
Cover Design by Miladinka Milic
Formatting by Vanessa Mendozzi
Publishing Consultant Linda Diggle

All rights reserved. Except as permitted under the Australian Copyright Act 1968 (for example, a fair dealing for the purposes of study, research, criticism or review), no part of this book may be reproduced, stored in a retrieval system, communicated or transmitted in any form or by means without written permission. All inquiries should be made to the publisher at the above address.

Disclaimer: Although the authors and publisher have made every effort to ensure the information in this book was correct at press time, the authors and publisher do not assume and hereby disclaim any liability to any party for any loss, damage, or disruption caused by errors or omissions, whether such errors or omissions result from negligence, accident, or any other cause.

A catalogue record for this book is available from the National Library of Australia

This book is dedicated to my family —
Liz, Tom, Melanie, Belinda, Robin and John (Nip.)

CONTENTS

Introduction	1
The warrior?	3
The Way	29
Discipline	47
Honesty	51
Spirit	53
Determination	55
Respect	57
Action	59
Now	63
Recycle	67
Change	71
Be on time	73
Show your neck	75
Stress	77
Make it count	81
Take massive action	85
Balance	87
Space	89
Fear	93
Connect	99
Money	103
Warrior tips	111
Introduction of the next book I am working on	119
Acknowledgements	123
About me	125
Appendix	127

INTRODUCTION

This book certainly has morphed since the beginning. With the success of my first book *Stand Tall*, it made sense to follow the same format for this one. But I found I had so much more to say on so many other parts of my life.

I covered the martial arts in detail in my first two books. But in this book they're just a foundation. I know I risk alienating my readers by delving into my time as a flight attendant and how it affected my life. But I decided to be open and honest, and not hold back. Because if I'm going to write about trust and courage and other timeless qualities then I need to be totally honest with you. It may be to my detriment, but I have to do it.

So this book has taken on a new focus. I have always wanted to write a self-help book, and the lessons that helped me were just too important not to share. This is the book that changed my life. It is the code that I lived by to achieve all that I have, body, mind and spirit. It does not matter where you are up to in your life. The *Warrior Upgrade* will help you.

I will start this journey at high school and then go into what it was like being a plumber. Finishing my six-year apprenticeship was an epic achievement, especially considering the suffering I experienced from the beginning. You may be thinking, *Six years? Aren't most apprenticeship only four?* Becoming a plumber, drainer, gasfitter and roofer takes a long time. There's three years of doing day release at TAFE, two years of night TAFE, and an extra year on top of that.

I recently recommended a plumber to my younger brother, and to my incredible surprise it was Matthew – an apprentice plumber who worked for the same company more than 40 years ago and is still working as a plumber all these years later. So as much as I disliked my job as a plumber, there are those who obviously love it.

As I said, I haven't made martial arts the focus of this book. There's so much more to my life, as you'll soon see. But there's no doubting the importance of martial arts in my life, and I've included some metaphors to get my point across in a way that makes sense to me.

Parkinson's now takes up a large part of my life. It keeps re-inventing itself, and my work is to be in the best shape possible so I can keep up with its ever-changing face. Parkinson's is different for everyone, and no two cases are the same.

I gain strength through my contact with the Michael J Fox Foundation, and Shake It Up Australia Foundation. They work tirelessly to fund a whole range of future treatment possibilities. Clyde Campbell, the founder of Shake It Up Australia Foundation, is a good bloke. He also has Parkinson's, so he knows exactly what it's like. I'm blessed that I have time in my day to write, and don't have the pressure of full-time work. I'm determined to keep teaching as much as I can for as long as I can.

A special "Thank you" to my family, including my sisters. While no family is perfect, we're all that we have, and so I intend to make the most of it.

I've also touched on the 'spiritual' side to my life (for want of a better term). For me, it's all quite straightforward. Nothing fancy or esoteric, although you may think otherwise after reading the introduction to my next book. It's quite 'out there'.

I think we've established a level of honesty between us now. The only way I can explain what I wrote is that it's part of me, and as clear to me today as it was when it first happened.

I've been careful with people's names, and in most cases have kept things on a first-name basis.

I'll now leave you to enjoy this short journey.

THE WARRIOR?

I've thought about this for many years. For me I think the idea of a warrior has morphed over the years to include anyone who wins over adversity. It's moral and honest. I liken the modern warrior to having certain qualities. Many of the qualities that I include in this book are classic characteristics that to me represent warriorship. But I'm no expert, and everyone is entitled to their opinion.

What defines a warrior? Is it a bloodthirsty gladiator? A calculated and calm samurai? Or is it a doctor or nurse working long hours to care for the sick without reward?

When you look at our history and try to define a warrior, we can often see a misguided notion that some dictators over the centuries are remembered as great warriors. The warrior is the person who stands up against these people or countries and refuses to be bullied.

So I now look on a warrior as someone who *doesn't* hurt another. It needed to change. It needed to evolve. Maybe if we can rethink what it means to be a warrior we can learn to live and teach how to live a peaceful life, a spiritual life, and we can follow the signposts so many great spiritual warriors have left for us over the centuries.

But therein lies another problem. Give someone a little power, and they weaponise their spirituality. How many people have been slaughtered in the name of religion over the centuries? There's no clear definition that defines what a warrior *is*. So all we can do is to say what it's *not*. (I've written some guidelines that might help.)

I'll first share with you a time when I was living in ignorance and heavily into fighting and hurting. There wasn't a great deal of softness around me. My fighting resembled a mad man intent on not giving an inch. I thought I was a warrior, but it was all purely a physical facade.

Then I fell all the way down, right back to the beginning. And I wallowed there until someone picked me up, lifted me onto their shoulders, and gave me a big shove forward.

This shove was important, as it broke my trajectory of misery. This is when I learned *"The Warrior Upgrade."*

Almost isn't good enough

The hardest and the best thing about warriorship is that it's long term. It needs to be integrated into your life, so it becomes a life style and not just a short course.

There are two important elements that are often overlooked in creating warriorship for life. The first is you need to make good choices long term, to the point where they become an ingrained habit. You can't just pay them lip service. Long term means every day for years – not just when you need it.

The other thing is there's no middle path. That leads to mediocre effort where you're not quite striking the goal. You must set your target and follow through with 100% every time.

So once again, you need to commit to the long term. This means creating master habits you enjoy and that empower you so they don't seem like any effort at all.

So these habits can be built up and reinforced over a period of months, if not years. I use martial arts as a good metaphor, as the grading system is great for developing long-term habits.

The second point is that almost isn't good enough. You'll find it difficult if you have this attitude. The slightest hesitation will have you spring boarded back to where you began and having to repeat the entire process again and again until you finally get it.

The first step
Taking that first step to recovery is the first step of warriorship. That's what this book is about – the road (or what I call "The way") back to health and beyond. But I must warn you. It's fraught with obstacles.

This book is about how I overcame everything in my way, and how you can use the same lessons to live a life as a modern warrior. I'd even go so far to say a modern spiritual warrior.

So, do you think that you're a warrior?

As I've said, there's no clear definition of what a warrior is. My take on it is that you must live to a code that's well defined. You need to have life experiences, maybe even some hardships, and push through them in a positive way.

And you don't hurt people. You help them.

Let's just cut all the excuses
Over the years I've taught thousands of people. And I've heard all the excuses as to why someone can or cannot do something. But it boils down to this: You'll only do what you feel is important to *you*.

No matter how busy you are, if what you're thinking of doing isn't a priority, you just won't do it.

I'm not going to waste your time (or mine) espousing fancy philosophy and using words like 'determination', 'courage' and 'respect' to try and motivate you. Because it won't make any difference unless you really, *really* want to do it.

And you usually get to this point when all else has failed – many times.

So, let's cut the excuses and get to the heart of the matter. If you want something badly enough, you'll find a way to make it happen. You'll find the time, the resources, and the courage to take action. You'll make it a priority, and do whatever it takes to achieve what you want.

So if you're ready to make a change and take control of your life, get ready to be shoved forward.

Pain is a great catalyst for change

Only when we've experienced enough emotional pain will we start to avoid situations that bring that pain back, and realise our current behaviour is making ourselves (and usually others) very unhappy. When this happens, there's just no hiding. You may have self-medicated with drugs or alcohol, or found other ways to run away from the pain. But it will catch up with you in the end, particularly if you keep avoiding the problem.

I'm now throwing you a lifeline. It's time to act.

Enough is enough

This book is for those who now realise that enough is enough, and change is the only option. I went through this process, and luckily came out the other side. So I'll be taking you on a journey of truth. And I hope you'll begin to find real determination and real courage on your own personal journey, and not just use the lessons as lip service without ever changing.

Before I started on my road to recovery, I never understood what I'd need to go through. It was only through this painful process that I began to understand and name the words and lessons that acted as signposts for me along the way.

This is the book I wish was available to help me on my healing journey.

There's the misguided assumption that we become wiser as we get older. But that's simply not true. The older we get, the more we're inclined to hang onto our old thinking patterns, habits and well-trodden emotions. Age does not equal wisdom.

We slip into aging, or rather, it creeps up on us, while we desperately hang onto any resemblance of our youth. And before we know it our family thinks they know what's best for us. We find ourselves exactly where we've been working all these years to avoid, checking into a mental health facility/hospital, retirement village or nursing home.

I sit here now, writing, thinking it will never happen to me. But it *did* happen to me. Everything changed in an instant. I went down very quickly, and my brother and Liz had to take control. They checked me into the Northside Hospital in picturesque Neutral Bay on Sydney's upper North Shore. That was the beginning of my long and painful climb back to what I thought was normal.

Trying to find happiness and contentment outside of yourself, and seeking answers in things and in other people's lives then wondering why it never lasts, is an exercise in futility. The peace and happiness you may be looking for is already within you. No-one is going to do it for you. We just need to turn down the noise in our head to be able to feel it.

Then it all comes down to choice. We can choose our attitude with everything we do. How this effects your life will be evident in how well you maintain your equilibrium in times of challenge and stress. Yes, happiness is a choice.

This book is a collection of motivators I've have put together that I used personally to overcome major personal limitations, and catapult me through adversity to peace, contentment and happiness.

We need to understand that we tell ourselves a story about who we are and what we stand for. It's usually a compelling narrative of negativity, and over the years it becomes a mantra that we repeat over and over again. It holds us back, convincing ourselves that it must be true and is the only truth.

How do we change this cycle? The first step is to just listen to it. Recognise that this voice inside your head doesn't have your best interests at heart. Challenge the narrative by asking simply "Is this true?" This will set in motion the next set of questions: "How do I change? And if I'm not my thoughts, then who am I?" When you get this far, you may be ready to finally take back control.

The 11th century Buddhist monk Atisha wrote: "The best scholar is one who has realized the meaning of 'no self'. The best monk is one that has tamed his own mind, the best quality is a great desire to benefit others, the best instruction is always to watch the mind, the best accomplishment is a steady lessening of negative emotions, the best generosity to non-attachment, the best discipline is a peaceful mind, the best wisdom is not to grasp at anything at all."

(I heard this on the *Sam Harris Waking Up* app.)

Nothing is going to challenge you more than the narrative you tell about yourself. It's totally your responsibility as to how you deal with it. You can live your life trapped by the limitations you believe define you. Or you can challenge the very nature of your being and constantly re-invent yourself with endless possibilities.

So how do you challenge the nature of your being? Well, I've put together the way I approached it so I could accomplish whatever I set my mind to.

As I've been involved in martial arts for many years, it's only natural for me to use that vehicle in some of my metaphors. But the book isn't just for martial arts folk. Everyone can learn from the following lessons.

I've looked at the strategies and ways of thinking I formulated to face the things I feared the most and still be able to keep moving forward.

It's hard to face your fears and limitations when the voice in your head is screaming out to stop. Regardless, you step into the unknown and pioneer a new path, where no one has ventured before you. After overcoming all challenges you finally rest, knowing you have achieved something extraordinary.

I like to think that I've lived a good life so far. I've followed my own path, and refused to live by other people's needs or expectations. I've learned the methods of the masters well in many aspects of life. And whenever I felt an urge or a need to change, I'd take those methods and set out on a journey to discover more for myself.

In a way, my disconnected parents gave me the greatest gift. They cared about me, but they cared more about themselves. I learned from a very young age that I couldn't rely on them, and so fending for myself was the only natural option. It wasn't a conscious decision. I just started looking after myself and it seemed quite natural.

I still wonder why I didn't share with my parents the challenges I was going through. Both of my parents have now passed away, and I don't see the need to drag them through another book. They did their best with what they were given, and I've forgiven them.

Making my own choices

I made the first decision to tread my own path when I was 12 by choosing to go to James Ruse, a selective high school in Sydney's North West. James Ruse was, and still is, the number one academic school in NSW. I don't remember sharing this decision with my parents, and I think I sent in the application without them knowing about it. If they'd paid any attention they would have realised that Normanhurst Boys High School was a much better option. It was literally at the end of my street, whereas James Ruse was nearly two hours away

I really wasn't suited to James Ruse, and I really didn't like going there. It had some real rough heads who got in because they had an older sibling or lived in the catchment area (the only way some of these no-hopers would ever get in). By the end of the first year most of these students were weeded out. But the ones who stayed were still trouble. Some would drink cough medicine and sniff liquid paper thinner just to get a high.

Most of us were under the power of Big Al, who fronted up on the first day of high school. He was more than six feet tall – a good head and shoulders above the other students in his class. He was a bully, and took pleasure in beating up the most vulnerable students. None of them deserved what he did to them. In the time I was at Ruse, Big Al just got bigger and stronger. And as he grew, his beatings became much worse.

I can still remember the relief of finishing Year 10, knowing I could leave all of it behind me. Unfortunately, I soon learned that bullying is everywhere, and that there's no safe sanctuary from it except in yourself.

Victor Frankl, who survived the death camps in Germany in World War II, writes in his classic book, *Man's Search for Meaning*:

"Everything can be taken from a man but one thing: the last of the human freedoms—to choose one's attitude in any given set of circumstances, to choose one's own way."

"When we are no longer able to change a situation, we are challenged to change ourselves."

At school, bullying was part of the culture, and I did what I could do to blend in and not bring any attention to myself. There was a large group of students who were very academic, and if you didn't try to keep up you soon ended up on the bottom. They taunted the rest by declaring they only did 30 minutes of study a day. Meanwhile, I was studying before school and for hours after school. I studied my ass off. Sometimes I did well, but most of the time I was just getting through.

To demonstrate the point, one year I came first in my class and 5th in my year in agriculture. The following year I didn't study as much and came last in both. The constant pressure took its toll.

I experienced my first bout of depression when I was 14. This led to a bad bout of insomnia the following year. For the life of me I just couldn't sleep, and I was always exhausted. My mother tried everything – honey and cider vinegar, and even a tot of port. I only started sleeping again when I stopped caring. This inadvertently reduced the anxiety, and I finally started sleeping again.

My older brother Rob was working at McDonald's at this stage, and when I turned 15 I also started working there. I loved it. I met many young adults from all over the area who went to all kinds of schools. Everyone got on and the camaraderie was great. It was a great relief after a day of school.

This was also the time I discovered beer. We'd all go out to the local pub at Waitara or to restaurants in Neutral Bay and North Sydney in a convoy of cars. I made so many new friends. Most of us were underage, but I was a tall 16-year-old and so I got away with it.

On one occasion I was doing a close at McDonald's, where you work back late after the store closes to clean and wash up everything. I must say that back then McDonald's was spotless. We finished around midnight, and the two people I was rostered on with said "Let's go down to the Cross," meaning Kings Cross.

Somehow I ended up in the back seat of a Datsun 120Y with 'Dalmatian' (because of his freckles) and 'Snoutsky' (because of his big nose), heading to Kings Cross. I was completely naïve, and had no idea where we were going or what we'd be doing there. I ended up in the front row of a strip club, and I was completely shocked. That was the end of my innocence.

We left just as the sun was rising and I had to get to school.

We drank a lot of beer. Back then there was no such thing as an allocated driver, and the police had only just started using breathalysers. So we all drank and drove. We had a great time, although I'm surprised there weren't more accidents.

Just before my 16th birthday I met my first love. She was also working at McDonald's, and she took a liking towards me. I was blown away. While she went to a Catholic school she certainly wasn't a prude. We spent a lot of time together, and she made me happy.

One day I called her at home out of the blue, only to find she wouldn't come to the phone. After it happened a few more times, I realised it was her way of breaking up with me. I was devastated. She cut me off completely, and I still have no idea why.

I kept working there for the rest of the year. I often wonder how much this affected my future relationships. It certainly affected my self-esteem and confidence, which took years to recover from.

Not surprisingly, I became a target for the McDonald's bully.

One night I spotted him changing out of his fancy shoes into his work shoes. As luck would have it, I also found some tubes of paint the marketing crew had been using. So while he was upstairs working I grabbed his shoes, filled them with paint, and waited.

Around 9:30pm I heard him scream from downstairs. Mission accomplished.

Once I left school I no longer had time for McDonald's. Despite being jilted by my first girlfriend, I really enjoyed the parties and going out. I learned a lot in a short period of time.

When I was 17 I made another decision. Once again it was a tough choice, but I just knew I needed to take my own stability and security seriously. I needed to be in control of my life.

I left the number one academic school in NSW to start a plumbing apprenticeship. The voice of Mr Clatworthy (then the maths master at James Ruse) still rings in my ear as he told me in front of the entire class, "Dickinson, you will be back". But deep inside I knew I was burning all my bridges and would never go back.

I can still remember the first day of my plumbing apprenticeship. I went to the company depot in Glebe (now a housing commission estate), but the business manager clearly wasn't expecting me. So he got me to sweep the floors and tidy up all the rubbish in the tearoom.

I realised this job was all wrong for me from the start. I hated it. But I kept on going. I had to. As a gift, my father gave me a cheap set of spanners that looked like those used by a car mechanic. But they were imperial instead of metric, which meant they were pretty much useless.

As I said, it was just all wrong from the start.

I often say nurses and plumbers have the dirtiest jobs. As a plumber you're dealing with water and sewerage – crap, crap and more crap. It's the worst job, and as a first-year apprentice you're always given the worst jobs to do.

I remember my father planting the first seeds about plumbing in my head (one of the rare times he showed any interest in me).

"Why don't you become a plumber?" he said. "It's a great job."

I lapped it up, enduring six hard years of a job I really hated just to get his approval. But it didn't make any difference.

So forget about seeking allusive approval or impressing a parent. It's a lesson in futility. What would they know anyway? You're far better not wasting your time and choosing what makes you happy.

It reminds me of a scene from the Will Farrell movie *Talladega Nights*. Young Will's father comes along to his school to talk about his job. But Will's mother and father are no longer together, and so Will rarely sees him.

Will's father upsets everyone, and is thrown out of the school. As the school security guards throw him onto the street Will yells out, "But why, Dad?"

"Just remember, son. If you are not first you are last."

Will goes on to become a NASCAR champion, driven by the last time he saw his father. He wins, loses, crashes, and suffers terribly in his attempt to live up to what his father said when he was a boy.

Years later, his family tries to reconcile at a restaurant. And his father ends up being kicked out of the restaurant.

"But Dad, I spent my entire life living what you told me," Will says. "'If you are not first you are last'. Do you remember?"

In reply his father says, "Hell, son. I was high as a kite and I don't remember what I said. You should not have listened to me".

By the end of the day I was so over it, not knowing what was coming next. I went to the office to clock off.

And that's where I met Jim Reynolds.

Jim was a loud, slightly rotund cockney man who swore every second word. He had a mop of straw-coloured hair and was slightly tanned. He wore stubbies that just hung off his hips, he sucked the life out of cigarettes one after another.

But his laugh was infectious, and I liked him a lot.

He was the supervisor at the site where I would work. He said, "I will take the boy". And that was it – I'd found a home for the next eight months.

I don't know quite what I was expecting. But I soon realised that as a first-year apprentice I was the dregs and almost insignificant.

There were real culture differences on the building sites I worked on. Depending on the type and scale of the job, some work crews were made up entirely of a particular nationality. That was fine, but the one thing that was totally different and out of place was their toilet habits.

We put an order in for 100 toilets, and like all toilets they had two parts – the pan and the cistern. The pan is the white part of the toilet that you sit on, while the cistern connects to both the pan and the water supply that washes everything away.

We ordered the toilet pans weeks in advance, and stored them in a dark corner on the second floor so they wouldn't get damaged.

That meant the only 'toilets' in the new block were these new pans waiting to be installed.

When the time finally came to install the toilets, the stench was so bad it almost knocked me over. I've often said being a plumber is a dirty, filthy job, and that being a plumber's apprentice makes it even worse. Well, these foreign workers had created their own private toilet block using the uninstalled toilet pans. They just crapped in them until they were full, and then moved on to the next. And because they weren't connected to the water supply, everything just sat there for weeks.

I now had a new job – carrying the shit- and paper-filled pans outside to hose them out, disinfect and clean them, and get them ready for installation. It was disgusting, but I was the boy and so it became my responsibility, the tradesmen laughing as I cleaned the mess.

Of course, the men who'd been using the 'toilets' didn't think they were doing anything wrong. They even complained about me moving their 'toilets'.

I clearly remember my first day of plumbing school at Meadowbank Technical College. It was a far cry from James Ruse, and it was hard to believe I'd gone from one of Sydney's most academic schools to plumbers school in just six weeks.

As it turned out, it was also the teacher's first day of teaching at TAFE. (Before that, Mr Guthrie had been working for himself.) And being a TAFE teacher back then was no easy task, especially when some of the boys simply refused to do the work.

Back then, apprenticeships were mainly for students who weren't very academic and had flunked out at school. So they were generally considered 'no-hopers'. Anyone who wasn't clever enough to get through high school did a trade.

It's a far cry from how things are today. Becoming a tradie gives you a high level of status, and with many trades you still need to complete Year 12. Many trades now also have a large female interest, although I can't imagine why a woman would ever want to be a plumber.

Going from James Ruse to TAFE was quite a challenge for me. I was used to the competitiveness of a highly academic environment, and as hard as I tried I just didn't fit in with my new group of plumbing buddies. So I just kept turning up, kept a low profile, and did what I needed to do without bringing any attention to myself.

I was in and out of plumbing apprentice jobs for the best part of the six years it took to become a qualified plumber. I moved around, trying to get the best experience in every facet of plumbing.

All the bosses I worked for quickly saw my potential and used me as a money-making machine. I was cheap labour – making apprenticeship money but being charged out as a tradesman. It was a simple formula, and who cared if the boy burned out?

This cycle of misery started when I was 19. I was a third-year apprentice working for a plumber who specialised in building new houses. The industry was booming, and Neil, my boss, was contracted to Kimberly and Sterling homes all over Sydney.

It wasn't uncommon to start the day at his mansion on the upper North shore at 7am and then drive to the outskirts of Sydney. His trucks would all line up in his driveway and take turns loading up with copper pipe, copper fittings, and bags of plastic sewer fittings.

This was the best part of the day. We'd all banter with each other to see who'd been fired recently. (Neil had a nickname – "Sack 'em Jack" – because the employee turnover was so high.) We'd then head out to all corners of the city, arriving somewhere on the outskirts of Sydney around 9am.

I worked with a tradesman named Carl. He was an older man, and a good plumber. We spent many months on the new housing estates at Campbelltown, a good two-hour drive from where we'd started.

By the time we arrived I was usually busting for the toilet. Many of the building sites we worked on didn't have a toilet, and so I'd have to find a spot off the beaten track where I'd have some privacy and use the 'tradesman toilet'.

One day I grabbed some toilet paper from the truck, raced down past the side of the house, and bolted into thick bush behind it.

After finding the perfect rock to squat behind in peace, I took down my pants and let out a long sigh as I relieved myself.

But as I did, I had the strangest sensation someone was watching me.

I looked up, and to my horror realised I was squatting in someone's backyard. Hidden in the trees in front of me, a gentleman sat quietly on a balcony with a clear view of his overgrown backyard.

And then he waved to me.

I quickly finished, pulled up my shorts and ran back to the building site, leaving an unpleasant pile for him to clean up. Not my proudest moment.

Some days the boy and I (the apprentice) seemed to perform miracles. One stage of plumbing is the 'rough in', where you run 20mm copper pipe from the front boundary to the various outlets inside the house. The boy generally ran the pipe to the house, and I'd run the pipework inside the house. But the distance from the front boundary to the house could be anywhere up to 50 metres. And the pipework had to be dug in with a pick and shovel.

Once the boy finished this task, he'd install the galvanised gutter to the fascia that ran around the house. Without any safety precautions in place the boy had to balance two storeys up, run a string line so there was fall on the gutter brackets, then install the gutter. It was a death-defying balancing act.

We never had time to stop for lunch either. I always hoped that by the time the boy had finished I'd be rounding up my pipework. But it rarely worked out that way. Quite often he'd be too slow, and so I'd be there until nightfall doing his work as well.

And then I'd have to do it all again the following day.

I was hammered, stressed, and not coping very well. By 9am I'd already be on my fifth cigarette, and usually smoked a packet every day. I ate hamburgers and chips every day, and drank litres of Coke. At one stage my mother went over to the boss's place to complain about my condition.

On top of this I was running to the TAFE plumbing school three nights a week, but still expected to do a full day's work.

It was brutal, and sometimes impossible.

At the start of my fourth year I was partnered with a first-year apprentice. The builder set harsh deadlines and expected us, the plumbers, to finish the entire stage set for the day. Failing to do so would upset the entire build process, and so you had to finish if you wanted to keep your job.

Around this time we were trying to get a nine-day fortnight. I was quite vocal, and the boss didn't like it. He had around 20-30 plumbers working for him, and losing a day's work would severely disrupt his flow.

Even though it was now law, he didn't care. I went in one morning and he sacked me on the spot. (He had a fierce reputation for churning through employees.) He marched me off the premises, and I made my way home with my tail between my legs.

I'd worked for him, and poured my heart and soul into everything I did, for almost four years. So I was pretty upset about losing the job I'd worked so hard it.

Why was I so upset? As I mentioned earlier, it was tied to having a sense of pride and wanting to be good enough. There was an honour involved in doing a good day's work and being paid for it. It was about being honest, and being trusted to do the right thing *even when no-one was looking.*

What drove me? I don't really know. It was like running a marathon as a sprint every day while having no idea where the finish line was. Was it the threat of losing my job? Or was it part of my personality – a sense of perfectionism – that compelled me to finish?

I suffered immensely through those times. I had no support whatsoever. And yet I was exhibiting qualities such as endurance, focus, determination and discipline without realising it. Maybe it was a misguided sense of wanting to be accepted, and to be okay.

I think I'd boxed myself into a corner. And it was all governed by fear. Fear I wouldn't get another job. Fear I wouldn't have enough money. And fear I'd never be enough.

Of course, these were just stories I told myself. As a boy I always catastrophised everything and looked at the worst-case scenario. I never knew any other way. No wonder it was so scary.

So I did what I thought was best. I picked myself up, dusted myself off, and thought about what I'd do next.

I approached a lot of plumbing firms for a job. But being a fourth-year apprentice made it hard. My wage was now close to a plumber's wage, which made it hard for an employer to make any money from me. But I had rent to pay, and so I had to find work somewhere.

It just so happened that Daryl Balkan, one of my TAFE mates, had an old Holden ute for sale, and he let me have it for $1,000. I then mocked up flyers for handyman work, along with some plumbing and gardening, and delivered them to postboxes and news boards in the hope of finding some work.

I was working for $5 per hour. Thanks, Daryl. You saved me, mate.

As it turned out, my father had a contact for someone who needed some gardening done. They lived on a large block of land in Western Sydney with two Great Danes. As I opened the front gate, two huge dogs the size of large, loping beasts came after me. I was terrified, and as they came running towards me I screamed and turned to run only to be saved just in time by the owner.

Then she showed me what she had in mind for gardening. The house was on an acre property, and everything was so overgrown it was practically a jungle. There was a good couple of months worth of clearing and cleaning work here.

A couple of weeks into the work, the wife and I got chatting. They had a self-contained apartment separate from their main property, and she told me the sink, bath and toilet were all blocking up.

Great, I thought. *Just what I need.*

So I went into plumber mode. And she was right. Everything *was* backing up.

I traced the pipework to a small septic tank near the building. After taking the lid off, I immediately knew what the problem was. The septic tank was completely blocked with swollen used condoms.

There was no way I was going to clear *that* blockage, and so I told the wife what the problem was.

"That's strange," she said. "George and I don't use condoms."

It turned out her husband George had been using the apartment as an office, and was having an affair with the cleaner. Unfortunately, that put an end to my gardening job (and their marriage).

By the time I was 20 I'd had enough. I was desperate to have clean hands, and so I sat the yearly entrance exam for the public service. I soon found myself working in a suite in the Garden Island Ships drawing office and studying naval architecture at TAFE. I was about as far away as I could be from plumbing, and I did well in every aspect. I loved the maths, the drawing and the mechanical engineering (which I excelled at). But the public service mentality wasn't for me. It shrouded me in a bubble that suffocated me, and when my fellow workers talked about working there until retirement I realised that while working in an office was a good experience, it wasn't for me.

I got a job with a local Eastern Suburbs plumber. It was just me and him, and so we were very busy. A lot of the work was fixing dripping taps and blocked sinks and toilets in public housing. Most of the people in these places were desperate – the poorest of the poor. Many couldn't speak English, and a lot of them suffered from physical or mental ailments. Some tried to keep their places clean, but others just languished in filth.

The blocked toilets were the worst. One place in Surry Hills had the filthy, shitty waste of an entire block of units discharging into their bathroom (and later their entire apartment). There was a mountain of shit and paper, and I had to dig my way through it to find the problem.

In complete contrast, I'd say I renovated more than 100 bathrooms in the richest areas of Sydney – Rose Bay, Double Bay, and all the surrounding areas. The renovations needed to be precise, and I worked for some difficult people. One woman would constantly bend over in front of the workers without any undies on. Another man would stand naked at his back door as the tradesmen shuffled past him pretending not to notice.

I remember renovating a bathroom, and using an electric jack hammer to dig up the floor. The apartment below would usually have what's known as a false ceiling, giving me some room to move. But I suddenly felt the jackhammer go limp, and it eventually slipped out of my fingers and dropped through the floor. Poking my head through the hole I'd just created, I discovered there was no false ceiling and the slab I was jack hammering was the ceiling of the apartment below.

The table and chairs below were covered in broken concrete, while a ray of sunshine caught the settling dust. A woman was holding s small dog, her face covered in muck and dust, her bottom lip starting to quiver. As the initial shock subsided she began to lose it. And who could blame her? Fortunately, the builder had the skills to fix it. But I'll never forget her face, purple with anger.

In the time I worked for this plumber I'd often see a new cars or van that he'd just bought. He'd also disappear for days at a time after loading me up and pushing me to work harder and harder. He was a sarcastic prick, and he refused to call me by my first name. The entire time I worked for him he called me Bruce, as in Bruce Lee. But I had to put up with it, as I still needed to complete six years working as a plumber.

As soon as I got my plumber's license I left him, and his business closed down soon after. Apparently I'd been his family's main source of income for months.

After six years and a lot of heartache, I finally started working for myself. I'd survived the bullying, and all the dickhead bosses and tradesmen I'd encountered over the years.

I worked for myself for six months. I also worked as a bouncer and doorman at one of Sydney's exclusive clubs, and taught martial arts at City Gym. I was very choosy about the plumbing work I took on. No more blocked or messy drains for me.

In the same six-month period I successfully applied for a job as a flight attendant with Qantas. And so, on 27th September 1987, my life changed completely.

And for a time I loved it.

There's great money in plumbing, and I thought about that a lot as I was leaving it behind. But I couldn't justify the money with the difficulty of the work.

One thing I haven't talked about yet was having to crawl under houses and buildings. I once worked on a job at Granville. I was still an apprentice, and working with a plumber named Peter Jones who wasn't well liked by the other plumbers and apprentices. My heart missed a beat as I saw him drive up on his Kawasaki motorbike.

On this job I had to crawl through dark and dingy spaces to cut out old, galvanised water pipes and replace them with copper pipes. And sometimes I had to tunnel through walls to get access to the pipes. It was hot and dirty work.

Peter was a large, well-built European man. I'd worked with him before, and knew he was both argumentative and aggressive. To make things worse I think he fancied me, and he constantly made sexual hints and innuendo. I ignored him, but I could tell his so-called innocent shoving and wrestling was allowing him to take liberties with his touching.

Fortunately I was well trained by that stage, and more than capable of looking after myself.

Peter was very strong, and he liked to wrestle me on the sand that covers the ground. But then he crossed the line, and that was enough. He touched me inappropriately, and I responded by shoving him away quite hard. The play was over, and it got very serious very quickly. He'd been warned. But I still had to watch my back because there was a good chance he would try to jump me again. I felt incredibly vulnerable, and it made me realise that men can also be subject to sexual assault especially when there's no-one around to watch their back.

I was so glad to leave it all behind.

I haven't always been such an honourable guy. My early role models were a philandering father, and an uncle who passed on the message that it's okay to have your cake and eat it too. My mother had a steady flow of boyfriends, and I did my best to stay away from them.

Too shy in my teens to understand what it all meant, it wasn't until I joined Qantas as a flight attendant that I came into my own. I had complete freedom to do whatever I wanted. My mother and father had approved of my behaviour without even realising it.

This was more than a young man just going through the process of sowing his seeds. It was like a kid in a candy store coming of age. Like everything I do, I applied a misguided determination with charm and plenty of trial and error.

Before I knew it I had friends all over the world. And even though I was sometimes in a relationship at home, I didn't see anything wrong with what I was doing. I was away, and figured no-one would ever know what I was doing.

But deep down I knew, and over time that would make all the difference.

As a flight attendant, I met new people every time I went away. But I wasn't outgoing. In fact, I was very shy. I feel the need to point out that the flirting was always just innocent fun, and the boundaries were always clearly set and respected by all involved. But I still didn't see anything wrong with it, even though it clearly wasn't normal.

Just to give you an idea about what the flight attendant did, here's what happened on a standard flight. You joined the passengers on board the plane, who were generally full of fun and enjoying the chance to be looked after. You gave them a drink, a meal, and then the lights would go out and they would sleep for a while. Later you would wake them up with a juice and breakfast, and then prepare everything for the plane's arrival. So the staff feeding you the day before would be the same staff waking you up in the morning.

There were some sorry sights on those mornings. But as crew we had to put on our happy faces. Quite often the crew would have had only a couple of hours off, and may have slept. I must have been a sight, as I didn't sleep on the aircraft. I usually crammed myself into an economy class seat allocated for the crew rest. (Some flights had bunks in the tail of the aircraft, but they were designed for small people.) Flying was exhausting, and the lack of sleep added up over time. But it was an incredible culture, and the people I worked with were such an interesting group of people. Towards the end of my flying career, when it was obvious I was over it, I did my best to disappear as soon as the meal service finished. I'd find a spare business class seat, pull a blanket up over my head, and hide from the crew.

I've spent many hours of therapy undoing the 'why' of my actions. The psychologists, psychotherapists and psychiatrists I saw were all keen to give me a label. It was simply that more was better, and I was enjoying myself.

I started dating my fellow workers. Who was to say that what I was doing was wrong? Most of my friends at work cheered each other on. We were all the same. It was just good clean fun, and no-one was getting hurt (at least not physically). Morals? Karma? I wasn't interested in any of it. I was the king of my life, and I was loving it.

(What I'm about to talk about took place more than 30 years ago. I was in a completely different space in my life.)

Enter a world of pain.

It didn't happen overnight. I thought I was in love. And I guess I was, or as much as you can be with someone you're having a fling with. But love was the last thing on my mind. The entire situation was like a shit bomb going off in my face. I tore my life apart.

I came home from work one afternoon to find my clothes strewn up and down the street. They'd all been thrown from the upstairs balcony. I gathered them up and checked into a cheap hotel nearby. I was now homeless, and unable to access any of my stuff. I was driving an old car I couldn't get out of second gear, and one point away from losing my driver's license for 12 months.

I was also being sued for $750,000 by a disgruntled ex-student who claimed to have injured his back in one of my classes. After six long months of defending myself, he didn't show up for the court date and the case was thrown out.

Just as the ink was settling on the court papers, the owner of the popular karate cardio program (yes, there's an actual business that combines karate with exercise) sent me a letter from his solicitor asking me to remove the words 'Karate and exercise' from a trademark application I'd applied for.

The gist of the application was to provide details on the type of kickboxing program I was trying to trademark. I'd said that it included boxing, karate and kickboxing. I thought 'Karate exercise' was just a generic term for 'fun karate'.

I was more than happy to remove the words. But I was totally aghast when the owner sent me a bill for $1,250 for me to pay for his legal bill. I refused to pay it at first. But letters of demand soon followed with more costs from his legal team.

I employed my own solicitor, and before I knew it I was $10,000 in the red. My solicitor explained that to defend it in court would cost at least $40,000, and even then there was no guarantee of success. So I stopped the legal process in its tracks, and paid both my solicitor and Karate exercise $5,000. A good lesson, but a very costly one.

To make things even worse, my ex and I were negotiating a financial settlement – never an easy discussion. And the solicitor I chose turned out to be a crime solicitor rather than a family law solicitor, although he didn't bother telling me until we were well into the negotiations. I kept on saying the settlement needed to be fair and equitable, and it was.

It was an extremely challenging time. But I'd brought it all on myself. But despite the intense guilt I felt for getting myself into this situation, it seemed I wasn't quite done with the pain.

Even after everything that happened, I obviously hadn't experienced enough pain. The woman at the centre of this pushed and pulled my strings in this 'on again, off again' spiral of emotional torment. I'd definitely jumped out of the frying pan and into the fire. Looking back, I added to the pain of my marriage breaking up and avoided all feelings that would have helped me heal by immediately jumping into another relationship – a dysfunctional relationship that added to the ocean of pain I was already experiencing.

The relationship didn't last, and I was soon back to my old tricks. I needed time to heal, and to make sense of this maelstrom of pain and suffering I was carrying around with me. But I didn't. I quickly went into another relationship. I was useless to my new partner as I was emotionally void – a wreck. It lasted 18 months before she threw her hands in the air and ended the relationship.

I'd now hit rock bottom

I was distraught. Yet another relationship had failed, and all the accumulated anxiety and pain I'd unwittingly gathered tarnished my view on what was really going on. For months the relationship had been like trying to fit a square peg into a round hole. Surely the depth of pain I felt wasn't congruent with what ended up being a breakup for the better.

I continued spiralling down into a place that would consume me. Before I knew it I was in the midst of a depressive breakdown. Now there was no avoiding the pain I'd never dealt with and healing that had gone unchecked for the best part of 10 years. In the end it became too much to bear. I couldn't get out of bed, and spent days curled up in the darkness.

You're probably wondering how it could happen to me. On the outside was this incredibly strong and focused martial arts guy who seemed invincible, and for years that worked for me. But on the inside, cracks began to appear. Like any proud man, I chose to ignore the warning signs. I was working two jobs (one of which was a night shift), had a young family, and was up to my eyeballs in debt. I completely blew my marriage, and ended up in a small one-bedroom unit with only an old futon I'd managed to salvage. (I eventually managed to take out a 'Buy now, pay later' loan so I could buy another piece of furniture.)

By this time, my marriage was over and I'd churned through a couple of very volatile relationships. I now understand the frustration my ex-partners felt. I thought I was over my marriage. But I wasn't, and I'd now become a commitment-phobe who refused to go any deeper than dating. It must have been hard for them. They were ready to settle down, but I was nowhere near it.

Eventually I'd come to realise that it was all slowly adding up – the marriage breakup, and the other kicks I was getting along the way. But I refused to stop and heal.

And then it all came together in a massive crescendo.

I went to my regular doctor and he said, "You're depressed. Take these drugs and you'll feel better". I was in seriously bad shape.

I can't remember the name of the drug, but it was definitely an anti-depressant. Almost immediately I started tasting metal and having trouble passing urine. But the drug had no effect on my mood whatsoever. In fact, I was getting worse.

My brother Robin, and Liz (who became both my saviour and my wife), got me an appointment at Northside Clinic. But first I needed to get a referral, which turned out to be no easy task.

Enter doctor number two. By this stage I'd hit rock bottom and was experiencing a complete depressive breakdown. I felt I'd completely lost my identity (what I like to call 'negative enlightenment'). I stayed in bed all day, just existing – an empty shell. Whoever I thought I was had disappeared, and I was left in the void. I had no idea how or when I was going to recover.

My mother just told me to cheer up. *Yeah. Good one.*

Sitting in the doctor's office, I was stunned when he refused to write me a referral to Northside Clinic. He said there was nothing wrong with me, and that I was just a little blue after my breakup. In the end he wrote the referral, but made it very clear he didn't think I needed it, literally throwing it across his desk.

Almost 20 years ago, I was wearing a hospital gown and patiently lining up to receive my daily medication. For the first 24 hours after I was admitted, I was put on suicide watch. Someone checked on me every 15 minutes throughout the night.

There were some seriously ill people lining up – bipolar, schizophrenic, major ADHD, PTSD, and all other kinds of anxiety disorders. At first I couldn't believe I was in the same line, and felt I didn't belong there. It was funny, or so I thought at the time. It reminded me of a scene from *One flew over the cuckoo's nest* where everyone waited in line for their morning medication.

This was my first morning at Northside Clinic. I'd been admitted the day before, much to my reluctance. I didn't think there was anything wrong with me. By the time I was lining up on the third day, I was fitting right in as the medications started taking effect.

So there I was in the line receiving the anti-psychotic drug *Seroquel*, which immediately affected my vision. But I persisted. I was also given the relatively newer drug *Pristiq*, which led to loss of libido and weight gain.

With the great support and help of Liz, my brother Rob, and the incredible staff at the clinic, I checked out after 10 days.

What became obvious to me was the number of people with serious mental health issues, and how debilitating those issues can be. Many patients had reached the stage where shock treatment was their only option. I can only hope I was not heading there, as it seemed a little severe. That being said, it seemed to be quite effective going by the results I saw. Many of the patients were regulars at the clinic and knew each other from past stays.

The nights were out of control. One night an elderly woman screamed as the assistants tried to control her. She had faeces all over her, and was throwing it at everyone and everything – not a pretty sight. The next morning she stood in line for her medication, cleaned up and medicated, as if nothing had happened the night before.

I was still a long way from being healed. But the clinic doctors thought I was well enough to continue my healing process at home. So I went home with a bag of medication and continued the slow healing process.

The one and only time my father reached out was when he dropped everything to look after me for a month where he lived with his wife Gayle (my loving stepmother).

With regular therapy, and the support of a couple of doctors, I remained in a holding pattern that can only be described as an anxiety fog. My medication was changed to *Lexapro*, and then to *Cymbalta* for the last 5 years of my experience with anti-depression and anxiety medication. (Feel free to google the side effects of these medications.)

The medical profession is good at getting you back on your feet and holding you there with pills. They're happy for you to sit in limbo and just survive. But I knew I wanted to heal completely.

Despite everything that had happened, I came to a point where I needed to decide whether the light at the end of the tunnel was still a train heading towards me or a way forward to calmer waters. So I made a conscious decision to start building a new life for myself. I'd hurt myself and others enough.

Once I'd made the decision to completely recover, I landed on my feet and quickly got on with rebuilding my life.

Here's how I did it.

I came up with a great business idea that completely re shaped how martial arts is presented and taught. I'd experienced rock bottom, and knew I never wanted to go there again. I worked long and hard, and loved every minute of it. I started with three students, and build the school to 1,100 active members. I bought another house and paid it off quickly.

And I eventually sold the business.

You may be wondering why I sold such a great business that I loved. The key is to not love it too much. Always remember that business is just that: business. It was always my plan, and selling the business didn't mean I was giving up martial arts. I was freeing up my time to be more involved with writing, blogging, and setting up an online presence for all my teachings.

THE WAY

What qualities allowed me to keep going when my mind was screaming out for me to stop? I've called this section of the book 'The Way'. It's a term commonly used in martial arts as in 'The way of karate' or 'The way of judo'. It loosely relates the journey to being on a path or road to personal discovery. It's also aligned with the way of the warrior.

'The Way' is a well-trodden track walked by many others before you. But over the years I've walked both on and off this path, and have never arrived at the end point. Yes, I've achieved some impressive goals. But deep down there was always an emptiness – a feeling that this path will never give me answers. Whenever I set myself a goal I'd work systematically until I achieved it. But when I *did* achieve it, I was always left with an empty feeling – a feeling there was something more.

But if not the path, then what?

Following a path gives the impression you're setting out with intent and expect to arrive and then possibly accomplish the desired result. On the surface it's all plausible, and the outcome seems logical. But do we need a path to achieve an outcome?

In my e-book *Lighting the Path* I go as far as saying the true master of 'The way' won't drag you from the front along the path, demanding that you follow. Instead they'll walk beside you, illuminating the path with their life force, chi or ki so you can navigate it safely and avoid the pitfalls and desires of the ego.

But on this path the ego always desires results, especially when it comes to martial arts. 'The way' is so much more than martial arts has to offer. It's a fearless and courageous approach to life in all aspects – mind, body and spirit. There's nothing to seek because you already have, and are, everything you need.

You've probably heard all the following subjects before. They've been well thrashed out by the range of life coaches and self-help gurus. Everything I'm writing here is just a rehashed version of what's been written before, except I'm digging deep from actual experience to give you my version.

Your mind grabs hold of it and wants to believe in its wisdom. But the real wisdom is being able to choose the rope from the snake that continually presents itself on the way. Everything in this book is designed to act as signposts to wisdom.

Wisdom is having and developing the tools to recognise truth from untruth. It may be handy, and you may find it useful. I've used this content over and over again, and refined it many times.

And I'm sharing it with you because it works.

I always apply my bullshit meter to make sure I'm talking from my truth and experience. And I expect you to do the same. As I've said, all the knowledge you need is already within you. The signposts in this book are designed to clear the clutter so you can clearly see awareness and stillness, which is always there and will always be.

What follows is what I've distilled from years of ups and downs. At times I didn't know I was using these strategies in their current form because I didn't have names for them. But by stripping them back to their basics and using them as part of my rebuilding process, I can honestly say they were the cement that held me together.

Will you be my guru?

Where do we draw the line as to what constitutes a 'guru'? It's a term often used to indicate someone has had a spiritual awakening of sorts. But how do we measure that? Over history, many gurus have attracted large followings. But these 'gurus' often start believing their own press, and take on a charismatic fervour that seemingly gives them the right to abuse, bully and take advantage of their followers. No religious or spiritual group is exempt. But I'm not going to point any fingers, as we're all on our own path.

These spiritual awakening can be quite varied, ranging from a partial transient experience of oneness to a complete and permanent dissolution of one's ego. People who've had a spiritual experience are in no way perfect. Just like everyone else they have things they need to work on. It's why there are so many stories of gurus who are still fighting their more worldly urges, particularly behind closed doors. The actual experiences of enlightenment/ spiritual awakening or self-realisation are all the same. And they can happen in an instant, or slowly over months or years. A good way to see just how far someone has evolved spiritually is to see how they live their everyday life and interact with the rest of humanity. The guru demonstrates wisdom and uses the world as their working surface to improve the quality of their self-realisation. But sitting in mediation for hours every day doesn't necessarily mean you'll understand the workings of the mind and achieve oneness and/or stillness in the noise we repeatedly regurgitate in our mind. Anyone can think themselves into anything.

And therein lies the danger. So many people out there put themselves forward as being enlightened, and they really believe it. Their actions may give the impression they've attained an element of oneness. But dig a little deeper and the cracks start to appear. It's best to avoid spiritual institutions and stick to your own counsel. Let's touch on karma. Karma is generated by action. According to the Vedanta scriptures (which are thousands of years old), karma is brought forward from your past life/lives into your current life. So in our current lives we may need to pay back a karmic debt accumulated from previous experiences. In its simplest explanation, this would explain why some people are enlightened in this life with no apparent effort, while others live their entire lives in spiritual servitude with seemingly no awakening at all.

But that doesn't mean their life has been a waste. They're living a good life full of wisdom, and burning samskaras that accumulate negative karma.

Whatever you believe, all negative and/or immoral action will hinder your path to a spiritual awakening. Looking for the good, and celebrating the connection that binds us to one another, is good. How does learning martial arts help us or hinder us in attaining a non-religious spiritual experience that can improve all aspects of our lives – mind, body and spirit? First up, by doing the simple practices in the classes – the bowing, the ready stance, the use of the ous response – we're laying the foundation to a more mindful and aware experience. No matter what's said to us, we slowly learn to not react. We learn to be calm. We learn to monitor our thoughts, and choose the path with peace at its centre. Over time, the reactive and angry choice that may have been a part of your programming for years is moved to a place where you can still see it but is now far enough away that's is no longer a set pattern you choose unconsciously. I don't think you ever get rid of these ingrained habitual patterns. But we can certainly keep them at arm's length.

It's certainly worked for me. I was angry for a long time, but I haven't had an angry thought for many years. And that's great. Having an angry demeanour will just eat you up. And it's the opposite of living an awakened life.

Be careful of cults

The alarm bells should have gone off the moment I stepped across the threshold.

It was just the warmth and attention I was given. The person I met at the door even knew my name. The room was spotless and quiet. I was excited as the room slowly filled with people. I could just feel I had nothing in common with others coming to this meeting hoping for answers to some of life's quintessential questions like "Who am I?" and "Why am I?" The poster that drew me in spoke to me in so many ways. I was well and truly sold before I stepped onto the premises.

I seemed like a perfect fit. It was either that or they'd done a slick sales job on me. From the beginning the school (as they liked to call themselves) seemed organised and had a well-defined structure in place, except nothing was written down and they discouraged you from taking notes. I was keen to learn the meditation, and followed their excuses as to why the process was taking so long, like a donkey following a carrot.

Instead, they encouraged us to use a technique called 'Be here now' (a simple mindfulness technique) until we showed we could reach a level of awareness that would qualify us to be initiated into the deeper meditation training. We'd repeat the same theme of lessons over and over again, hoping the powers-that-be believed our awareness level was worthy of access to their well-guarded meditation practise.

In the meantime, we were lectured on a combination of philosophy, Shakespeare and the lessons of Vedanta passed down from a mysterious Indian guru (referred to as 'His Holiness' by the school's principal who was the only one allowed to have direct access to 'his holiness').

The heads of the school kept this little white lie close to their chest, among many other subtle things that were starting to not add up. But in the meantime I followed on blindly week to week, month to month, year to year. Whenever I questioned a senior tutor about how I was feeling, I'd be told it was just my ego, and that I needed to be more attentive and try harder.

Finally, after several years, my group was being initiated into meditation. We were told the school principal had chosen a special sacred mantra for each student, and we were instructed not to repeat it to anyone. I found this strange, as Peter the school principal had never spoken to me (he didn't even know my name) and yet he was choosing a special sacred mantra for me based on my personality and other hidden secret criterion. But I felt special and privileged, and so didn't question the process. I trusted them.

It's not that things were bad. Looking back, I'd say things were slowly creeping up on me without me realising. There was more pressure to attend the classes, attend the retreats, and help with the general upkeep of the school.

Service was a huge part of running the school, and helped keep costs to a minimum. I can see the value in service. It's their version of the Karma Yoga practised in some yoga schools. It's not slave labour but rather a way of doing things for the common good, contributing while being aware of what's coming up for you. In the end, you always have a choice.

For me, things started falling apart when the elderly headmaster Peter passed away. From what I can make out, after he died a couple of senior tutors went to India to establish a link with His Holiness. (I still do not know his name.) But they found there was never a solid connection with Peter and he never had permission to initiate people on His Holiness's behalf, which made the whole thing a sham built on lies. It was also revealed that everyone initiated into the meditation received the same mantra. No wonder we had to keep it secret!

It was time for me to leave. As the school was scrambling to stay alive, many of the so-called advanced students I looked up to started behaving like children. All the talk on ego and all the spiritual lessons just went out the door. I went to a couple of meetings with senior members, and the arguing and bickering between them all was embarrassing.

I walked away.

The school's reaction was to keep going as if nothing had happened. I was with the school for almost 10 years, and I left without a word.

Was I in a cult? I don't think so. Was it strange? Yes, very much so. Meditation should never be a means of control. If needs to be open and transparent, without any secrets. These days, everything you need to know is on the internet. I was sucked in for years by the promise of something wonderful. But in hindsight, staying at the school did nothing for my spiritual growth. I don't feel my time there was wasted, but their version of developing spirituality is not for me.

After I left the school, I jumped out of the frying pan and into the fire. I studied with the world-renowned Satyananda Yoga school. I went on several retreats at their ashram at mangrove mountain, and in the beginning I loved it. But their dark and murky past eventually caught up with them. This once great yoga tradition was ripped apart by the royal commission into abuse against ashram devotees.

I was there when the ashram fell apart. The senior swamis all ran for the hills, pleading ignorance to anything that may have gone on when they were part of the ashram. The ashram was closed, and sold to pay out the many claims of abuse by the leaders stretching back 30 years. There was even talk that the founder and his son who currently oversees the remnants of the tradition knew what had gone on.

It's such a shame. There was nothing like the ashram anywhere else. It was special, and I really enjoyed my time there.

But now I no longer have any connection with that particular yoga school other than the chanting I do every morning. I would also like to say that my teacher was an important part of my healing process and from what I know had no part in the downfall of the Ashram.

I remember an interesting man who was my tutor and mentor at a school I attended for some years. He often talked about the mind, and the importance of bringing presence into your mind and into your life. He was adamant that the mind was slippery and couldn't be trusted. He then introduced me to the school's style of meditation.

While I deeply respected him, we fell out of communication after I left the school. I often asked people about his wellbeing, and though he was older he seemed quite well. I was sure he'd be walking his talk and living a good life as a spiritual warrior.

One morning late last year in 2022, I had a strong urge to see whether he was okay. I spoke to one of his closest friends, and they told me he'd cleaned his apartment, put on his best suit, left a long letter, and then climbed to the top of his apartment building and jumped off.

At first I was simply horrified. *Why?* I just couldn't fathom the pain he must have been in. He was having trouble walking and experiencing other ailments. He also lived alone, and didn't get many visits from friends. I'm still upset by it all. All those years of spiritual work could not save him. I think he was just ready (he was in his early 80s), and probably ran out of puff.

How do I feel about it now? I keep thinking *How could he?* Especially after listening to him lecture for hours on the power of the mind. Did his mind get the better of him? Unfortunately, I'll never know.

He was a good man, and I'm sure he thought it through. In the end he chose the time for his demise.

Goodbye, warrior. And thank you for all the lessons. I'll miss you, John.

It's so common for people in a position of spiritual power to abuse their position. Nothing surprises me now. But just because someone has personal insights into the nature of life doesn't mean they have their shit together. Quite often the opposite is true. They start believing they're special, and abuse their position thinking it's normal.

The example that probably shocked me the most was a late Tibetan master who had quite a following here in Australia. He was a renowned author, and had a huge worldwide organisation. It turned out he was abusing and bullying many of the women. This is just one example of many who get caught with their fingers in the cookie jar. These so-called spiritual masters aren't exempt from being human.

I am very careful these days to whom I give my attention to. I do not attend any spiritual groups, or retreats. I listen to podcasts that I am interested in and follow meditation teachers that have been around for years. But mostly with my meditation, I set a timer and sit in stillness and watch my thoughts rise and disappear. It is as simple and as complex as that.

Rope or a snake

I first heard this great analogy in the modern spiritual classic *I am That* by Sri Nisargadatta Maharaj. And it changed my life.

Fear and anxiety can be crippling. Living a life ruled by fear is suffering. Most of what we fear is just an illusion, and what we fear never eventuates. But at the time, those fears seem incredibly real. So how can we differentiate whether the fear is valid?

A really good way of looking at this is the 'rope or the snake' analogy.

Imagine you're walking down a bush track, and you think you see a snake. You become petrified and panic, because it may well be a snake.

But the following day you walk along the same track, and you see a coiled rope on the path. You then realise that in the dark you mistook the rope for a snake. But it *looked* like a snake, and so your entire being went into overdrive preparing to deal with the situation.

If you'd just stopped, taken a breath, and looked and listened, you would have seen it was just a rope. It was the illusion, and the thoughts created by that illusion, that caused all the distress and suffering. This same process happens continually throughout the day. We form opinions, judgements and ideas around just about everything. Our lives are ruled by our habitual patterns – the same thoughts and habits just repeating themselves repeatedly. It's a bit like the movie *Groundhog Day*, a great comedy about life repeating itself. Our identities are forged from these repeating patterns, but they're all just castles in the sand.

We hold onto our identity with all our strength. But what is it really? A hotchpotch of random thoughts that try to give us a firm footing. How much of our energy is taken up daily believing the rope is a snake, and that our thoughts are the truth and serving our best interests?

Have you ever followed a thought with your awareness? Tried to see where the thought came from and where it goes? You'll soon realise they're totally random, and disappear without a trace as soon as you start scrutinising them.

But the illusion can be very powerful. I know this all too well, having been in its grip for most of my life. Being so busy that I never had any time to just stop and 'be'. I lived on adrenaline, and was always stressed. It was easy for me to bang elbows with people and end up in conflict, but I just put my head in and kept pushing.

But then life then caught up with me, and I changed.

The first sign was the softness that came to my training. Giving, not forcing. I also stopped trying to predict every outcome, and started to let things take their natural course.

I was able to feel and discover what was real for me, and I settled down into living with a clear purpose. My blood pressure went right down, the underlying anxiety disappeared, and I could now clearly see the rope and not the snake.

Anxiety

Anxiety has a habit of creeping up on you. It could be part of a constant backdrop to how we relate to the rest of the world. We're unaware of its power, but it can be there without us realising, influencing everything we do and making us wonder why we're under so much stress.

I could clearly see the power of anxiety on meditation retreats, particularly 10-day silent retreats. During these retreats there was no contact with the outside world. No mobile phones, no computers, no Netflix, just meditation. It gave me the opportunity to completely release without any influence from my mind.

And my anxiety reduced to zero. I'd forgotten how it felt to be normal. In fact, it was a real eye opener seeing just how much anxiety was influencing my life. Everything I did was being filtered through a constant low-level anxious state of mind without me realising it.

I first came to understand just how much anxiety plays on our lives near the end of the meditation retreat. I picked up a book with low levels of violence, and I could feel the anxiety creeping back. It was very subtle, like stepping into a comfortable shoe, ready and waiting.

We live in a constant state of unrealised stress. And unless we take measures to counteract it, it will increase a little more every day. For example, being bombarded with media and getting upset at what we see will eventually have a negative effect on us.

How much we choose to take on in these somewhat difficult times is up to us. But unless we take serious action to control our stress and anxiety (or at least become aware of it), it will eventually affect our health both mentally and physically. Learning a simple meditative practice to help you release yourself from the power of your thoughts is a good idea.

You don't need to go to a meditation retreat, as you can access many of these skills right here and right now. But it takes effort and persistence to learn a new way of behaviour. Even if you think you're stress- and anxiety-free, exercise for the mind, body and spirit will still help you. The advice to "stop and smell the roses" is worth noting. Release into the power of the present moment, and stop constantly running your life with thoughts of the past and the future. If you keep running from one event to the next without paying attention, your life will just waste away.

Simple things I do to keep me anxiety-free

Get out of bed as soon as you wake up (unless it's the middle of the night). Don't sleep in and allow your thinking to over-exaggerate things.

Mornings were the one time I needed to be disciplined. It's easy to get caught in a negative loop. If you feel it happening, just get up and meditate. If you're having trouble sleeping, focus on someone else and use the 'loving kindness' mantra (the last meditation in my online meditation course) to take the focus off yourself. Aim for up to 30 minutes a day doing mindfulness or meditation.

→ **Exercise.**
Choose something that gets your heart going and you puffing. Include some lighter exercise such as yoga, Pilates, tai chi

or chi gong. Practice mindful meditation the moment you wake up. I now practice meditation at least twice each day.

→ **Eat well.**
Eat less. Medium fat, low carb, lots of leafy greens, fibre, plenty of raw green smoothies and lots of water. Limit your dairy, keep your bowels open. Don't be afraid to take a gentle laxative (but check with your doctor first). I now eat a modified Mediterranean diet.

→ **Limit the booze.**
I often have one glass of red wine with dinner. I also aim to have no drinks for at least 2 days a week.

→ **Don't isolate.**
Reach out to friends and family. I know there is always 'stuff' with families but connect as best you can. Try not to make it all about you. Look for ways you can help others.

Your cave

For a while, my beaten-up Mitsubishi Lancer was my home. I tried to find a small apartment to live in, but I couldn't get a break. I had no rental history, which made it really hard to find a suitable property.

One day I went to an open house for a block of units that had just opened after being renovated. I immediately recognised the real estate agent. He was an ex-flight attendant, and we always got on. He said I could have whichever apartment I liked, and so I chose a neat one-bedroom with views. And it wasn't long before I was unpacking the Lancer and moving in.

The first thing I needed to really start healing was to get my home in order. The security of having a roof over my head allowed me to set up a base camp of sorts. Over the years it became obvious just how much I needed to make that commitment to myself.

What I'm trying to say is I wanted leverage on myself to succeed. And it worked.

I spent months looking for the right house to buy. Many of the local real estate agents knew me by name, and would often call me if they needed an estimate on a house price. I was determined, and nothing was going to get in my way.

I applied the same science I used for getting my black belt to finding the right house to live in. I've always believed you make money on a property when you buy it. My first house was a derelict terrace house in Glebe that I found a couple of days after it fell through at auction. I snapped it up for $230,000, and while it had great city views it was a complete mess. It was practically uninhabitable. But I applied all the building skills I'd learned over the years as a plumber and bathroom renovator, and turned it into a palace.

Unfortunately, I lost that house in the divorce.

I've never tried using property to create wealth. I think it messes with people's lives. Everyone deserves to have four walls and a roof over their head. It's a fundamental right as far as I'm concerned. But when property is used as an investment, people become pawns in the investors game.

When I flew for Qantas, I used to sit in the crew seat at the back of the aircraft. As we came in to land in Sydney, I'd block out entire streets with my thumb. People would work a lifetime to pay off their house, and yet I could block it out with my thumb.

In the meantime, I rented the small one-bedroom unit and set it up as my war room. I covered the walls with butcher's paper. I was getting ready.

I found my second house in much the same way as the first. My real estate friend called me a week after the house did not sell at auction and said it was mine if I wanted it. It was a classic California bungalow with incredible art deco trimmings, and it eventually became my castle. I spent years renovating it, and later built a training studio out the back.

Buying a house gave me a tangible goal of working hard to pay it off. You may not be able to afford a house, and to be honest I couldn't really afford it either. But I kept working hard, and eventually paid it off. And believe me, after all the torment of completing a plumber's apprenticeship, I knew what working hard meant.

Things were going smoothly at this point. But in October 2016 I was hit with another major challenge.

I kept being reassured by several doctors (one psychiatrist, two neurologists, and a doctor who specialised in psychotherapy) there was nothing wrong with me. According to them I was just being hypervigilant about my health (the new way to describe hypochondria) and suffering from anxiety. "Just keep taking the drugs and you'll be fine," they said. But I was slowly losing my dexterity and movement in my arm.

I was eventually diagnosed with early onset Parkinson's disease.

It was such a relief to finally know what was wrong. I'd been having odd symptoms for almost 10 years. Now I could finally get my life back into some sort of order. (Anxiety and depression are early symptoms of PD.)

I now had a strong home life, and despite Parkinson's I felt the most stable I'd been in years. And so I decided it was time to finally come off the final antidepressant: Cymbalta.

Cymbalta numbs your emotions, and you forget what it's like to feel normal. And while it keeps the lows at bay, it means you no longer feel the highs. And I knew getting off it would be a meaningful way to finish that chapter of my life.

Slaying the tiger

In order to slay the tiger, you have to feed with the pigs.

This is one of my favourite sayings. In order to achieve what you want, you may have to get dirty in the trenches.

I'd tried getting off it a couple of times before. But because you can't break up a capsule like you can a tablet, your only option is to go from the 60mg dose to the 30mg dose, and then from the 30mg dose to nothing. In the end the fatigue and head zaps became unbearable, and I started taking it again.

But this time I had a plan.

Over a six-week period I transitioned to the 30mg dose. I then asked my doctor to write me a script for a 20mg dose. Screwing up his face, he resisted and said I'd be fine going from 30mg to nothing. But I was adamant. "No," I said. "Please write me a script for a 20mg dose, and I'll get it made up at a compound chemist." (I'd already spoken with the chemist who was totally supportive.)

In the end I got my script, and spent another two months transitioning to the 20mg dose.

I went to the same doctor to get a script for a 10mg dose, and got the same resistance. But I dug my heels in and got the script.

It took another six weeks to transition to the 10mg dose. I'd take one every Monday, Wednesday and Friday, and nothing for the rest of the week. Unfortunately, it's something you can't rush.

I liken Cymbalta to an alien that has attached its tentacles to your brain. It refuses to relinquish control, and so you need to slowly and gently lull it to sleep.

I understand that antidepressants and anti-anxiety medications have their place. But if you think you're well and stable enough (and have the support of your family and a good doctor) get off Cymbalta. It's an insidious and addictive drug that changes your brain chemistry. And it's so damn difficult to stop.

Liz

There's only so much our partners/wives/husbands can take. Your life, and what you do with it, can have a huge impact on your family.

I first met Liz in 1998 – about the same time my life started to unravel. And even though she liked me, she wisely kept me at arm's length. We stayed in touch, and for years she quietly watched my back. She was there for me as I started to heal and get my life back together. She watched me struggle from one dysfunctional relationship to the next when the answer had been in front of me all along. Liz loved me, and continues to love me, with all her heart. I'd never felt this depth of love before, and so I couldn't help but to fall in love with her. Liz and I got married in 2018, and we've built a life together based on love and mutual respect.

I've left my old life behind completely. Liz has made it very clear that my previous behaviour has no place in our relationship. I've had a strong moral compass my entire life, although at times it was pointing north while I was moving south. Mind you, some of the world's greatest and most creative people have led turbulent lives. And they didn't always act in a way that was conducive to their chosen path.

Fortunately, I've learned from the error of my ways. The methods I used to fight back are what this book is all about. And I'm being been honest about it all because I don't want you making the same mistakes.

I was lucky to have people close to me who could see the spiral I was in.

I don't blame anyone for how my life turned out or hold anyone responsible. I'm happy, at peace, and blessed to think I may be helping you because you're reading this and seeing things from another angle.

One thing I've learned is that trying to find happiness and contentment in money, food, booze, drugs and other stuff is like living on a razor's edge. One slip can really hurt you. And if you keep falling down and getting up again you just end up with more and more cuts.

The peace and contentment you may be alluding to is within you. It always has been, and always will be. This may sound a little bit 'new age', but once you get the idea you can stop being the victim and work on taking control of your life.

Nothing will challenge you more than the story you tell yourself about yourself. It's your reality. We tend to live by this story, and it repeats itself over and over. How you deal with it is completely up to you. If you want to, you can live your life trapped by the limitations you believe define you. Or you can challenge the very nature of your being and keep reinventing yourself with endless possibilities.

Don't just give this lip service and say, "Yeah, I get it," because you don't. Over the years I've taught these simple skills to thousands of people. And you know what? People rarely assimilate them into their lives. To have lasting change you need to build the emotional muscles that will sustain you long term. Start now, and be one of the rare individuals who has the courage to venture beyond the anthill.

DISCIPLINE

While I was disciplined in my training, I clearly wasn't disciplined in anything else. I didn't do drugs, and only had the occasional drink. But I certainly had discipline issues when it came to women and relationships.

There are different types of discipline. It's not an overriding quality that envelops every aspect of your life automatically. You may be a great sportsman but have a lousy diet. You may think you have a solid grip on your life, but find you're always running late. We need to recognise the weaker aspects of our lives, and use the stronger, more disciplined aspects of our lives as a template to improve them. Do that, and you'll slowly strengthen the areas that need work.

Assuming you really want to.

I've always liked this Tony Robbins quote: "You will only change when the pain of not changing is overwhelming". When you've reached the end of your tether, and changing is literally the only option you have left. If you keep repeating the same patterns of negative behaviour you'll never change, and you'll keep wondering why everything is going against you.

Without discipline, you'll never achieve anything.

I taught martial arts for more than 30 years. And in that time I saw plenty of people walk through the doors. I'm often asked how long the average student stays. To be honest, not very long.

It takes at least 2-3 years to get a black belt, and I've graded well over 250 students to that level over the past 15 years.

It seems most people aren't into anything long term because it involves constant self-discipline. Whether it's daily exercise, diet or a relationship, maintaining excellence and personal standards involves making a minimum commitment to self-discipline. You're the only one who can do it. No-one else can do it for you. If you never achieve what you set out to do, and constantly fall short of where you want to be, you may need to re-examine your habitual process.

Self-discipline doesn't mean denying yourself some short-term gratification to earn a greater prize. For example, losing weight isn't the hard part of going on a diet. The hard part is maintaining a lifestyle where you can keep the weight off and stay healthy long term.

Aiming high is fine. And having a resolution that you'll stay committed to your goal no matter what a great start is. Here are some pointers to help you.

- Work within your means.
- Set small tasks that can grow with time.
- You'll never keep it up if you start with the bar set too high.
- Don't just give in if you 'fall off the wagon'.
- It's okay to take a few steps forward and then back.
- Recycle then renew.

Over the years I've seen many students stop training because they missed a couple of weeks. They consider themselves failures because they feel they've missed out on too much. When I first started my own training, a senior student told me that if you quit you'll never pick it up again. That's the biggest load of bullshit I've ever heard, but it's what many people hear, think and ultimately believe.

Make it long term
Long term is easier to work with, and far more enjoyable. A lot of people suffer from 'firecracker syndrome' (a short, intense period of terrific enthusiasm that quickly comes to an abrupt end)

whenever they start an activity.

It took me years to get my diet right, I just couldn't do it all at once. Get the facts about what's healthy. (Fortunately there's plenty of information available online these days.) Don't go cold turkey, just slowly start reducing the bad stuff.

And the same goes for just about anything else.

Create a habit of small daily disciplines, and work on them a little at a time. It's the small wins that give you the confidence to improve and test the boundaries of your limitations. Doing your daily disciplines over days, weeks, months and years has a cumulative effect, slowly wearing down those negative habits. But as the word itself suggests, it requires discipline.

An example of my daily disciplines

These are pretty basic, and you can adjust them to suit. I use variations of these. Having a morning ritual of a few daily disciplines will help you start every day in a positive way.

1. **Get up and move.** Try some basic stretching, yoga, Tai Chi or Chi Gong. It doesn't need to be complicated. Just keep it simple.

2. **Meditate.** Leave your phone and other devices off until you have moved and meditated. Start at 30 seconds and build up from there.

3. **Take a mid-morning, 60-second recharge.** Just stop, turn away from whatever you're doing and breathe into your stomach. Expand your stomach as you inhale, and contract it as you exhale.

4. **Increase your heart rate for at least 30 minutes three to five times a week.** Walk fast, jog, swim or cycle. Your body will love you for it. If you haven't exercised for a while, talk to your doctor about it first.

5. **The last thing you think about before you sleep will be the first thing you think about when you wake up.** So be careful how you finish the day.

When to quit

Sometimes quitting is the best option. If it's not giving you joy and happiness, or it's no longer empowering you or anyone else involved, then the path may no longer have a heart and it might be time to move on.

HONESTY

So many people don't tell the truth. Great words spray out of their mouth, but they never back them up. I understand this may seem a little *too* simple, but it lies at the heart of success. Your word is law, and people will only trust you if they believe you will keep your word.

This is where it can all break down. Throwing out statements without following through seems to have become the norm. But saying you'll do something and then actually doing it is a revelation.

Make it a cornerstone of how you live. It will elevate you beyond mediocrity, and set the stage for a remarkable life. But doing it every time and no matter what takes discipline. It's so simple to blurt something out to fill a gap in the conversation or make someone feel good. But if you keep forgetting about your commitments and ignoring the implications, you'll soon get a reputation for being hard to believe.

Having a reputation for keeping your word is one of your greatest gifts. As poet John Lydgate once said, you can't please all of the people all of the time. And sometimes the truth can be very painful. But it's better to be upfront and honest so people know where they stand.

SPIRIT

Spirit is not something that you just automatically have. It really depends on the person as to just how much they can tolerate. And you will never really know or understand your spirit until you are challenged. Only then will your resolve be challenged and you will be able to see what you have. This may or may not be a physical challenge. It could also be a mental or spiritual challenge. Once you get an idea of how much you can tolerate you will build what I call spirit muscle. This then enables you to choose wisely the challenges that you want to take on. It is a choice to just give in at the beginning of a task. You can easily talk your way out of anything.

Warrior spirit has connotations of fighting on the battlefield and distinguishing yourself in combat. But unless you are in the army, the closest you will get to a battlefield is in combat sports, which range from boxing to UFC, with an entire range of not so extreme martial sports in between. We can also say that sports like rugby have a warrior feel about them. How do we bring this warrior spirit attitude into our lives without having to prove ourselves on the battle field? Spirit is just one of the legs that encompasses warriorship. It goes hand in hand with courage, self discipline and determination. Spirit encourages us to just keep going, put one foot in front of the other, dig deep, and then dig deep again. It may mean that we have to endure pain or painful situations.

An example of this was when I was living and training in Japan. In the dojo we had to sit in seiza. This means sitting on our knees. I never got used to this and was usually in considerable pain after even 5 minutes of sitting. We would be expected to sit in seiza whenever an explanation was given, and sometimes the explanation would go on for ever. Quite often I would lose all feeling in my legs and would need help to stand up and move. This was a real test of spirit. My legs would scream out in pain but I would just push through it. We all have times when we have just had enough. Every little win makes us that little bit stronger for the next time. But life was not meant to be a constant struggle. These days, I am learning to now quit a little sooner.

DETERMINATION

Determination is probably the one quality to have above all others. It's the 'secret sauce'. Why do some people show more determination than others? To start with, you need to align your potential with what you want to achieve. Determination and potential are two of the secret ingredients for reaching your goals.

A new student joined my son's high school when he was in Year 9. The student was a good sprinter, and played well on the wing in rugby. He immediately caught the eye of the athletics coach, who could see tremendous potential in him. The coach did a great job of nurturing this potential with his determination.

The student went on to become:

- school champion
- Combined Associated Schools (CAS) champion
- state champion
- Australian champion.

He also represented Australia at the Commonwealth Games, World Championships and Olympic Games.

Being in tune with your potential and trying to find the 'sweet spot' is often where we fall short. We aim either too low or too high. If we aim too low, we may become despondent and lose our 'vision'. And if we aim too high, we may end up falling short and be left wondering why we never seem to get ahead.

A critical step is to make sure we're doing and following what we believe is right for us. (Some people think this just means having a positive attitude. But it's so much more than that.) Many of us don't have a trainer to motivate us, and so it's all up to us. We navigate the path alone. This means firmly setting our moral compass, then heading out to face whatever challenges life throws at us along the way. It also means taking the knocks, bruises and bumps as you keep putting one foot in front of the other.

Over time you learn to go beyond your perceived barriers. You start to believe you can succeed regardless of your current situation. Use the small wins in your life to prepare yourself for the big challenges. Sometimes a tiny flicker of hope is enough to keep you putting one foot in front of the other. Challenge yourself constantly by facing new fears.

RESPECT

This is one of the legs that holds martial arts. Respect is not demanded. It is passed down from student to student and is an integral part of the structure of the dojo. The art of bowing separates the wood from the chaff. By lowering your head you are in fact showing trust to the other person. If you do not have a code of respect in the dojo, then the essence of martial arts is slowly and surely lost.

That intrinsic truth that is interlaced into all the movement must remain and be practised with diligence if you are going to call yourself a martial artist. It is just too easy to not make the effort or to fool yourself that the respect that you practise in the dojo is enough. If you are not committed to it, it will slowly waste away, like anything else that is not practised.

Respect in martial arts can be difficult to understand let alone practise especially if there is no one to demonstrate it correctly. Respect is the glue that separates martial arts from other sports. It is so unique and needs to be valued. Bowing is not a subservient act, it is a powerful act that binds us on the warrior path together. In so many classes the warrior act of bowing has been sadly replaced for a high five or a fist pump. This removes all warriorship from the dojo. How can you even think about developing killer instinct when the real fighting traditions have been removed.

With no respect there is no zanshin, with no zanshin there is no awareness and with no awareness, balance is not broken.

So how does someone that has never entered a martial arts dojo develop and practise respect? Well, the last thing that I want you to do is to start bowing indiscriminately.

Everyone deserves to be respected. Start by being polite to everyone you come into contact with. Whether it is a waiter, cleaner or some one that collects your garbage, just be polite. When someone cuts you off in traffic or bumps you in a super market. Don't react as you usually would, don't take offence. Move to avoid trouble and smile.

ACTION

One thing I'm particular about is taking immediate action. Procrastination is the rust of the mind. People are amazed at how quickly I get things done. I set my life up in projects, and do a little bit every day. If you're running a business and can't answer your emails in five minutes then you're just too busy.

When I ran my martial arts schools I had anywhere up to five office staff. The entire day was set out on a one-page checklist, and I expected everyone follow it. But it was a difficult protocol to get right, as those who worked in my office always had an excuse as to why they didn't follow it. For example, they would say; "I've memorised the process, so I don't need to mark off the checklist." But that was bullshit, and they always ended up making mistakes. Running a business with more than 1,200 members and still having time in your day relied on a level of exactness.

On the checklist, enquiries took priority over everything else. If the phone rang, the staff had to drop whatever they were doing and answer it. People were always amazed at how quickly we answered the phone.

My philosophy has always been enquiries come first. I wanted them booked in and committed to a trial class before they could even think about calling another school. I'm amazed at people who spend a small fortune on marketing and advertising but then take forever to respond to enquiries.

This simple process was a cornerstone of my business success.

Taking action also goes hand in hand with not putting anything off that needs doing. I used to avoid issues that weren't urgent, or that I knew were important. But I always needed to act eventually to avoid fines and having my bank accounts closed.

In 2022 I needed to close down some company names that were no longer relevant. I could see they were just sitting there, and that I needed to change the company name on one of my main accounts. But I just put it off and ignored it.

Big mistake.

The bank gave me eight weeks to reinstate the company or they'd close the account and take all the money. So I had to approach ASIC (where the company registration lived) and arrange to reinstate the company. Only then could I remove the money from the account and close the company down again.

Dealing with ASIC and the bank was a nightmare, and I suspect the time and energy it took was a hangover from COVID. I knew the company was needed to keep the funds available in the account. But I kept putting it off until the entire situation imploded. So if you need to do or say something, just get it done.

I often have a lot of personal projects as well – organising a holiday, writing this book, weeding the garden, running a competition, and so on. But I never try to do too much. I simply work systematically on them a little every day.

I used to be a real goal setter – stressing myself out trying to complete unrealistic goals in impossible timeframes. But I wasn't enjoying the journey or giving myself any room to relax, and so I just gave up.

I stopped setting goals. Instead I came up with concepts and plenty of alternatives. I allowed a sense of grace to take over, and naturally gravitated to things I wanted to achieve and that felt right for me. Once I allowed stillness in my life, and reduced the mental clutter, I could just feel what was right for me. It became effortless, and things just naturally fell into place. I wasn't lazing around, expecting things to just happen. But I wasn't wasting time on things that would be too much work and grind away at me either.

Once I felt the right path, I acted on it immediately. This process will make a lot more sense if you try to live a mindful life and use stillness as your reference.

The Japanese find a spiritual significance in the falling of the cherry blossom petal. It blossoms so vibrantly. Its nature is to be as beautiful as it can for such a brief speck of time. Then it falls, and its short life of brilliance is over.

The cherry blossom is a celebration of life, and it's the same divine spark we all share. Just as quickly as its life begins, it is over.

As I venture along this incredible journey, I'm acutely aware of the sand running out. I've faced my mortality once before. It was too soon, and I wasn't ready. When will we ever be ready? There's only one place where that fear can't grow in power – here and now.

Embrace the moment with passion. Turn your face to the wind and feel the power of nature. We're all are part of it. Face fear with love and forgiveness.

Action vs reaction

If you stop to think about it, most of our interactions are totally reactive. The action has already happened, and we're too slow to see it happen. What we want to develop is the ability to be there as it happens or, better still, just before it happens. We can then respond with insight and wisdom.

The aim is to be able to include it in our daily practises. We can start by meditating with a mantra, or simply observing the breath. With enough practise, we'll be able to observe our thoughts as they rise. We can then live ahead of the pack, never getting caught up in other people's agendas.

NOW

This small word can really pack a punch. Living now! It sounds like an easy thing to do, because if you're not living in the now then where and when *are* you living? In a practical sense that's true, but it's important not to confuse living with existing. While the body exists in a physical space, our thinking can easily stop us from being aware of that space.

We spend so much time planning our lives away that we forget to enjoy what we're doing right now. And our lives slowly disappear.

So while we exist in a space by default, the conditioned mind and habits can take us on a journey well away from where we are right now. Living now isn't wasting time thinking about the past regrets, or planning for an unrealistic future. We can learn to gently acknowledge the mind and its desire to be anywhere but in the present moment. Without criticism we come back to the task at hand, making a conscious decision to make friends with the here and now. It's not 'us versus them' and being here and now is *not* a competition. We need to gently woo the mind out of its slumber and guide it back to a trigger (such as the breath or body sensations) in the present moment.

I have tinnitus (ringing in the ears). And the quieter it gets, the more I become aware of the ringing. But behind the tinnitus is a calm stillness that's affected only by the noise or thinking that's layered over the top of it. The stillness is always there, and always will be. It's one thing that never changes. My aim is to relate from this place of stillness behind the thoughts, and not from my thinking. Yet even the slightest thought can have the stillness slip away.

We all carry around vast amounts of irrelevant stuff. It's usually stuff about the past that keeps us trapped in a continually rotating dialogue in our heads. If you're a meditator, or have tried to listen to the sounds around you or watch your breath, you'll know what I am talking about. There's a newness and freshness that recycles itself in every moment.

Each moment is a new experience that has never happened before. It takes courage to stop needing to control this moment, and the next, and the next. But it's exactly where life is happening. If you keep filling it with thoughts of the past and the future, you'll miss it. Your life will fly past, and you'll get to the end of it wondering what that was all about. As Sam Harris says, "The goal here is wisdom. The wisdom that comes from recognizing how things already are and stepping out of the fantasy life born from having a mind that is perpetually distracted".

I often ask my students, "How do we know when you're in the present moment?" It's when you're totally engaged in what you're doing and not thinking about what you're doing. When that happens, you're free to live your life as it unfolds without needing to control or manipulate it into what you want it to be.

Nothing will get done unless you really want it. Bringing presence into your life is the simplest way to make lasting change.

Bringing the present moment into your life
- Develop a light touch to life.
- Be curious about other people rather than critical.
- Lead with empathy instead of your story.
- Learn to listen and guide the conversation away from yourself.
- Ease your way back to the present moment using the senses.
- Listen to the quality of someone's voice. Just listen.
- Take time to *really* look at a flower.

- Feel the texture of the clothes on your skin.
- Taste your food. Slow down and *really* taste it.
- Pause between activities. Listen to the phone ring before answering it.
- Give attention to the working surface (e.g. your hands while washing up).
- Create a still space during the day by paying attention to your breath.

We've all have had to weather hard times. It's a part of life. Good and bad work off each other. Taoist philosophy says that to feel the good you must know or have felt the bad. No one wants bad, but you can't avoid it. It happens to us all eventually.

How to get the best outcome from a confrontation

Have you ever felt good during an argument or disagreement? Ever felt good getting angry, or getting your own way? There are no winners when you push your agenda to get your own way.

But how do you feel when it's over? Better, right?

I think we all want to live a happy, stress-free life. But an aggressive encounter can really mess up your day.

Pushing your own agenda, and getting stuck on being right or having the last say, is how conflict gets out of control. Wars last for years because men and women are squabbling. But it's rarely about the agenda. It's usually about the ego *driving* the agenda. We're all guilty of this. But if you don't address the driver you'll always be a slave to your thoughts. Here's a simple technique I use to defuse any uncomfortable situation I find myself in. That said, I rarely find myself arguing or in ego-driven disagreements. I hardly ever get angry, not because I avoid or deny it, but rather because I've replaced that with an icy stillness – neutral, non-reactive and, above all, present.

I always say, "The person who becomes present first in any altercation is the person who will have the best outcome". So how do we do this, especially when our ego is screaming out to be recognised?

The process is quite simple but does take practise. And it needs to happen quite fast – a standard practise for all martial arts.

The moment you feel a situation escalating, give your full attention to the other person's voice. Listen to the quality of it as you take a breath. By doing this you put your mindset into neutral, and create a small gap that connects you to the stillness.

From here you have a choice: engage, or let it go. Yes, you could just get angry. But putting your mind into neutral helps you see that getting angry might not be the best course of action. You effectively switch off habitual emotion you normally lose control of, whether it's anger or something else.

Simple, right?

So what stops people from doing it? Their ego, and their deep-seated desire to control others. Changing, or even wanting to change, takes discipline and courage and is the warriors way. And so we generally change only when we've experienced more pain than we can endure. But by then it can be too late, and you end up hurting yourself or others. If you're serious about wanting to change long term, I suggest learning a martial art that incorporates a mindful practise or simple meditation in its teaching.

RECYCLE

The beauty of living now is you can recycle and resume whenever you think about it. You can start again from the beginning, or continue from where you like. The key to success is to not berate yourself in any way. No judgement here. Just stay calm and start again.

This can be handy for things such as weight loss, and breaking other ingrained and not-so-healthy habits and addictions. It's easy to fall off the wagon and indulge in your favourite food. But this can bring on all kinds of emotions, particularly guilt.

Don't waste your time. Just start again. Set a plan, and stick to it. Accept the current version of you. It may not be your favourite version, but it's all you have for now.

THE BULLET TRAIN IN TOKYO, JAPAN

THE COLOSSEUM IN ROME

THE PARTHENON IN ATHENS, GREECE

DWARFED BY A MOUNTAIN IN AUSTRIA

THE BEAUTIFUL CHERRY BLOSSOMS IN TOKYO, JAPAN

INSIDE THE COLOSSEUM

TREKKING IN NEPAL. TOP OF THE WORLD

I LOVED GOING TO INDIA. IT HAD MY FAVOURITE TEA AND SPICE SHOP

THIS IS MY TRAVEL PERMIT FOR TREKKING IN NEPAL

CHANGE

Have you ever thought about impermanence? Put simply, everything changes. The great spiritual traditions, particularly Buddhism, has it as one of their cornerstone teachings. As soon as you get used to something, it changes.

Tibetan Monks spend hours creating beautiful images on footpaths using coloured sand. But once they're finished, they just let the wind blow their images away. The beauty of the image vanishes as if it never existed. It's a great reminder to appreciate beauty as it happens without trying to cling onto it.

I love the saying, "This too shall pass". Every experience you've ever encountered has passed. There's no discrimination as to what each one entailed. Every experience – good, bad or neutral – changes over time, and all you're left with is an image or a memory of it. Unfortunately, we usually forget the details, and so what we're left is a poor representation of what actually happened.

Trying to hold onto an experience is a sure way to prolong suffering. Clinging on to our memories and trying to re-live them robs us of the brilliance of creating new and exciting experiences, and healing from past traumas. I'm not saying we should forget the past. But we can celebrate it and then, over time, let it go.

Even the most iconic structures have crumbled to dust. The Roman Empire? Dust. The Berlin Wall? Dust. The Egyptian Empire, which lasted thousands of years? Almost dust. They were all magnificent, and destined to last forever.

Whether it's a great empire or a sunset, their beauty is simply a breath out. It came. We experienced it. And then it disappeared. We all die. We can't avoid turning to dust. It's inevitable. Samurai warriors lived their lives with death on their shoulder. They were often the bodyguards of great warlords, and knew they could be called on to face their mortality at any time.

Knowing this, they chose to see the beauty of life's experiences as they unfolded. Poetry, calligraphy and even the tea ceremony gave them a calm awareness.

We don't live as bodyguards in Japan. But like the samurai, we won't live forever. There's no need to obsess about it or get morbid. But we should at least bring it into our awareness. Having a healthy respect for our mortality makes understanding impermanence, and living every day as if it's your last, so much sweeter. The inspiration for this section came from a simple jigsaw puzzle that now sits completed on our dining room table. It's a beautiful picture. It's also the first jigsaw puzzle Liz and I have completed together, and so I feel the need to hang onto it. But just like the Tibetan sand images, I'll break it apart and let the memory blow away in the wind.

BE ON TIME

This may seem like a small unimportant point. This is something that you can work on immediately. Your time management is indicative in how you run your life. Some people are habitually late. I make it very clear on my Online Mastery Academy, I will not wait for you past the agreed time when we schedule in a zoom meeting. I don't care what you must go through or have been through in order to be on time.

Being on time starts the instant you get up in the morning. I am never late. There are plenty of applications and devices that we can use to effectively remind ourselves of our schedules. So many people still manage to sleep through their alarm. I find this incredible. Being on time is something real and tangible that you can work on now. It is hugely important in showing that you can keep your word. Being on time means you are willing to walk your talk.

SHOW YOUR NECK

I like this passage from the late Stephen Levine's *Embracing the Beloved*:

> *Wolves have an innate ability to limit aggression with certain body gestures. For instance, during even the most ferocious challenges, if one wolf bows his head and shows his neck to the other, the violence instantly ceases.*

Displaying the neck is a responder for peace, a sign of submission. It has occurred to us that another way the human mind has remained unevolved is in its general lack of deep responders, its capacity to violate another without mercy or any natural limitation of heartless behaviour. Just look at how far Americans will go to maintain their archaic and senseless gun laws.

Decide how far you'll go to get your point across. When does it stop being about what you want to say and become a baseless battle of the ego that quickly turns into deadly violence – uncontrolled and vicious. Look at the brawls taking place every day. What have you got in place to ensure you know when and how to back down?

STRESS

I'm now acutely aware of how much havoc stress can cause. When I'm under negative stress, it really flares up the Parkinson's symptoms. But when I'm doing something I really enjoy that might seem stressful, I'm well.

So stress isn't necessarily a bad thing. But if it becomes relentless, and affects your ability to reduce it, then it needs to be addressed. It can drag you further and further into a life filled with negative stress without you even realising. It only becomes evident when it starts affecting your health – physically and emotionally.

You may not be able to reduce the stress you're under through work, relationships or just running a busy life. But you *can* take steps to alleviate its effects – getting regular exercise, maintaining a healthy diet, establishing good sleeping patterns, and so on.

Reducing stress is a major factor in removing the clutter that chunks away your life. You'll have difficulty letting go if you can't see the wood from the trees. That is, being to let go of stuff that is right in front of you.

Anger

Anger is a by-product of stress. I've been more aware of getting angry at people who continually ask me what I'm saying. Parkinson's disease can affect how you speak, which makes situations involving loud spaces or talking on the phone especially difficult.

I'm finding I need more preparation. I write things down, and practice what I preach in being present, patient and mindful. I feel the anger rise in me and breathe through it.

A comment, a shove or even a sly look can be enough to set you off. It can take over in an instant, or slowly engulf you. Either way, that brain snap (or mind explosion, or whatever you want to call it) can change your life and the lives of others in an instant. You may be a rational and reasonable person, and appear to be in total control of your life. But when someone pushes your buttons who knows what's just below the surface?

You need to control your anger and your temper. If you don't, the damage it can to other people's lives, families and work can be immense. Mastery of anger management is indeed a huge step in mastery of self. When someone around you is angry, how bad do you feel?

Martial arts can be powerful. And the force needed to hurt another person is minimal. Developing the mind, creating stillness and space, and being neutral are all essential in your martial arts practice. It teaches you to observe the thoughts and emotions that arise during training (particularly during intense sparring or wrestling), and to not attach to emotions as they arise.

As an emotion such as anger arises, unless you monitor it with presence it will take over and you'll become the anger. It may only be for an instant, but in that instant you could inflict physical or emotional damage, or even be hurt yourself.

Of course, later you'll say things like "That's not like me" or "That was totally out of character". And the emotion will sleep until the next time it's awakened and acted upon without consciousness.

The power of words

The words you use can have an amazing effect on your communication. They can be perceived as hostile and quickly ignite a situation. So choose your words carefully, use them to show empathy rather than anger.

A perfect example is the Korean language, which is very abrupt. The meaning isn't rude or out of place, and it all sounds quite normal to Koreans. But if you're not familiar with Koreans or their language you can easily misinterpret what's being said.

As a flight attendant I flew to Seoul and back several times in an aircraft full of Korean passengers. For the most part they were excellent passengers. But they had very little patience and couldn't wait their turn. As soon as the aircraft touched down they'd be opening the overhead lockers and preparing to get off the plane. The crew would then have to sit them all down again – not an easy task. But I knew it was part of their culture, and that I needed to stay calm. I find it funny how Koreans and Japanese can be so geographically close yet worlds apart culturally.

MAKE IT COUNT

Our lives are always full. We have this preoccupation with 'doing' that keeps us busy. From the cocoon of our parents we step out into the world, and then quickly launch ourselves onto the treadmill of life. As our lives gain momentum, we keep zinging past events and moving onto something new. Whatever we just experienced quickly becomes a memory, and we stack it on top of all the other memories that fade into the backdrop of our thinking.

When does life take on more meaning? Is it when children are born? Or is it when their grandparents pass away? For most of us it takes a jolt, an intervention from the side, to shift us away from 'doing' and toward 'being'.

Don't get me wrong. 'Doing' is great for practical purposes – striving, goal setting, achieving, attaining, justifying, winning, losing, etc. But most of us just keep 'doing' because it's all there seems to be.

But 'being' releases you from that need to win, achieve or attain. You can still play the game, but you no longer care about outcome. It's a space where you can become more engaged in the process, and give each step the exact amount of effort necessary to complete the task in the most positive way. We often become so intent on getting the result that we stop enjoying the process.

In life we say things like "I'll be happy when I earn more", "I'll be free when the kids leave home", "I'll be more relaxed when the exams are out of the way". This is the conditioning of a mind forever trying to replace the current moment with a better one.

And it's one of the ego's biggest lies.

In truth there is *this* moment, complete and pure. And after that is the *next* moment, also complete and pure. And so on.

There's a great movie with Adam Sandler called *Click*. He's given a remote control that allows him to fast-forward through various events in his life. It literally lets him skip the parts of his life he doesn't enjoy so he can experience more of the moments that may bring him happiness. But the remote control soon learns his patterns, and starts fast-forwarding him through events it thinks he won't enjoy without him even pressing a button. He soon finds himself at his deathbed, and realises just how much he's missed out on because of all the fast-forwarding.

'Being' means 'letting go'.

"But," I hear you ask, "If I let go, who will I be?"

The truth is you'll be the same person you are now, but with a softer, lighter touch to life. Your attitudes, ideas and beliefs will still be there, but you'll have more room to observe your reactions to them. You'll become supple to your approach to life, and not so rigid and stuck in your ways.

Slow down, and make every moment in your life count. Make the most of every situation by choosing to 'be'. Take a moment to completely indulge in this. Let go of everything that's going on, just for a little while. Fully engage with what you're doing. When you lose yourself in 'being' you are truly present, and giving your full attention to whatever's in front of you that needs it.

Don't worry. All your 'stuff' will still be there. But when you practise this regularly, you slowly give power to being able to enjoy life's wonderful process as a journey rather than a destination.

Warning signs

Going full bore all the time slowly depletes your ability to be able cope. You need to schedule regular breaks on both a macro and micro level. Maintaining equilibrium requires a balanced life. Whenever I feel I'm pushing too hard in one direction, I'll temper it by choosing the opposite direction. Too much yang (hard training, hard living, fixed ways of thinking) must be counterbalanced with yin (soft training, time out, being flexible and forgiving.)

Here's an analogy I used to gauge how I was feeling and healing.

Imagine your state of mind is like a beach. Out past the breaking waves is the worst you could feel. It's dangerous, and the sea is rough and deep. You need help.

In the opposite direction, beyond the sand, is grass. And here you feel happy, safe and content. You can lie back in the sun, and all is good with the world.

It's where we want to get to.

The distance between the sand and the other side of the breaking waves is your journey. And as each day passes, little by little you move closer to the beach.

Here's how to give yourself regular breaks so you can recharge and regroup.

1. **Take some space each day to stop, breathe, and reflect on what's making you tense.** Take time each day to relax your shoulders, relax your face, breathe out, and let go of having to think. It can be as short or as long as you want. *You could also try my-30 second meditation to get started, or even my Mastery Academy.*

2. **Don't take everything so seriously.** Try laughing about things that would normally upset you.

3. **Look for the good.** Be careful what you let in. The world can be a harsh place if you let it. Seek out people and situations that nourish you, and avoid the people and situations that dump on you or bring you down.

4. **Forgive yourself, and let yourself off the hook.** We tend to be our own worst critics. It's okay to make mistakes. Just let them go and carry on.

5. **Worry can be debilitating, and goes hand in hand with anxiety.** For chronic worriers, constructive self-talk and a good therapist is a must. I regularly recite "The Serenity Prayer". (Google it. It's worth it.)

6. **Work out.** Make exercise a priority. It's easy to push it to the end of the day, and just as easy to make excuses for not doing it.

7. **Pay attention to your self-talk.** What are you saying to yourself? Our inner critic can be brutal sometimes. And how we speak to ourselves can be worse than how we'd speak to our worst enemy. Enough is enough. So start changing the dialogue, and don't accept anything that belittles you in any way.

TAKE MASSIVE ACTION

This is the closest I'll ever get to goal setting.

I have 20 levels of black belt, and have won several championships around the world. Over the years, through trial and error, I've been able to refine how I prepare for tests and competitions.

Here's the method I use to prepare for any challenge – business or personal.

1. Decide you want to do it
Take your time, think it through, and ask yourself this simple question: "Is this what I *really* want to do?" Don't get stuck in a job or situation you can't stand. I did, and it was such a waste of time.

2. Get leverage on yourself
Whenever I travelled somewhere to grade or compete, I'd buy non-refundable tickets. Think about ways you can give yourself an incentive to reach your goal.

3. Commit to your decision
Tell someone who will hold you to your commitment. You could also announce it at work or on social media. That way, you'll have to go ahead with it to avoid ending up with egg on your face.

4. Take immediate action
Do something that will solidify your intention. Make sure you:
- get all the information so you know exactly what's needed
- set a plan, and work within your time constraints
- work within your limitations (e.g. family, work, size, shape, age)

5. Be Consistent
I always try to do a little every day. Don't cram and try to do it all at once.

6. Get Fit
This is an important one. There is overwhelming evidence that now supports fitness for health. Remember: a fit body is a fit mind.

7. Visualise it
This is a huge part of my preparation. I do a lot of mental revision, visualising myself doing the techniques and getting them in the right order. It's great, and takes only a couple of minutes a day. (I usually do it to music.)

8. Work on your diet, nutrition, sleep and relaxation
Stay up to date. (There's plenty of information out there to help you.) But here's what you need to do in nutshell:
- Don't eat anything out of a packet.
- Have plenty of raw fruit and vegetables, fish and chicken.
- Drink plenty of water, and limit your tea and coffee intake.
- Watch the carbs.
- Moderate or even give booze a miss during the week.

9. Don't obsess over winning or the result
Whether you win, lose, pass or fail, you only really win if you did everything in your power to prepare.

10. Have fun
You need to do this more than anything else.

BALANCE

Martial arts are more than just physical movements. They're generally marketed as a way to life and health using mind, body and spirit. But most martial arts teachers fall short of the mark, and have no idea what the 'mind' or 'spirit' parts entail.

Mind training isn't just talking to yourself repeatedly and hoping it will change your habitual thinking patterns. Mind training goes much deeper, and questions who you think you are.

Our mental balance can be quite fragile. It can be broken by a look, a stare, a word or even a tone of voice. Think of how quickly friends can turn on you simply because they didn't like the way you spoke to them.

When it comes to martial arts, this is the real work. The physical side is easy, while the mental and emotional stuff can take years. But this is the *real* training, and it's far more valuable as a life skill than any self-defence move.

Teaching martial arts is difficult. It's easy to teach the physical stuff. But it's a lot harder to teach people about themselves, and help them realise their thinking is the source of all their suffering.

Going through the belt levels in martial arts can really test your emotional balance. Let's face it: If we can't handle a little mental pushing and shoving in the dojo, what chance do we have in real life? Do we come out a black belt, but without the emotional control we need to handle someone verbally abusing us, or accidentally cutting us off in their car?

If you quit because you don't like the way you're being spoken to then you've missed the biggest lesson. I teach martial arts, and I'll keep challenging the edges to bring my students to a higher awareness of themselves. Some will be lucky enough to understand the brilliance of this journey. But most will just complain, leave, and blame the vehicle of their growth as the problem.

Here are some things to think about.

1. All situations are neutral.
2. You can never know what another person is thinking.
3. Our egos keep growing, and our habits strengthen the older we get.
4. Try and not react. Instead, take one breath.
5. Go from no fuse and reacting immediately to having a fuse.
6. No-one can hurt your feelings. But your thoughts about it can.
7. The mind can justify anything, anywhere, at any time.
8. The present moment is your only real freedom. It's the only place and time life is actually happening.
9. Commit to learning more about who you really are.

SPACE

"You will not find the mind by looking for it. Mind has always been empty. There is no need to search. It is the very one who searches. Simply settle without distraction directly into the searcher."

– Patrul Rinpoche

We often hear the phrase 'taking the space'. Taken literally, it can mean seeing an opportunity where nothing currently exists, and taking up residence in that void. It can mean taking a spare parking space, or moving to an area of a crowded room that's relatively empty. And in business, the perfect plan for success is to find a niche no-one else is in, and develop your business within that space.

In martial arts, taking the space is a great way to become aware of the distance between you and your training partner or opponent. Once they move into that space you're monitoring, you can see their every action. This simple idea is also great for daily life, and reflects the metaphor of taking the space.

So whenever you're getting stressed, or there's a sense of uneasiness or conflict, try 'taking the space' by stepping back or away and putting some distance between you and whatever's going on. It could mean stopping everything and taking a couple of deep breathes. Or it could mean removing yourself from the situation completely and setting a new path for your life. The important thing is to allow yourself some distance, and this is where the space occurs.

Taking the physical space doesn't necessarily mean taking the mental or spiritual space. Quite often we create physical distance, but bring the same mental dialogue wherever we go. Still, taking the physical space is a great first step.

The beauty of taking the mental space is we don't necessarily need to remove ourselves from where we are or what we're doing.

You can take the mental space by simply changing your attitude. If you're stressed out at work because of deadlines, take the space by looking out the window. It doesn't matter what the weather's like. Just looking away from what's in front of you will help you create that mental space a few seconds at a time.

1. Understand there's a neutral space you can tap into.
2. This space can be mind, body or spirit.
3. The business space doesn't necessarily mean 'reinventing the wheel'. It could simply mean taking a better look at what you're already doing.
4. Take the physical space by removing yourself from aggressive situations. Choose not to get involved. It just creates more stress.
5. Create a space each day by doing what you really enjoy that totally removes you from your normal routines. For example, I'm a martial artist but also love tango dancing and studying Japanese.
6. Take the emotional space by living your truth in relationships. Ducking and weaving in relationships just creates more stress and wastes energy.
7. Take the mental space by taking several deep breaths regularly during the day.
8. Take space from your mind's constant internal dialogue by paying attention to your senses one at a time.

9. Take the moral space by walking your talk.
10. Take the spiritual space by learning mindfulness or learning to meditate.

We live in a world of reaction. We react to situations only after they've occurred. By walking the path, you create the presence and awareness to see situations as they evolve, and take action to ensure the best possible outcome. You start to feel things before you see or hear them.

FEAR

Fear is undoubtedly one of the main reasons we find ourselves stuck. Many people just roll along, happy with their lot, and never needing or wanting to challenge the outer edge of life. Walking the warrior path is not for these people. Walking the path is for people who have a desire or a need or are motivated by truth. The fear's always there. We just build a life around avoiding it as much as possible. Well, that and pain. After all, fear usually means pain.

Learning to accept fear as an innate part of our physical makeup takes practice and work. The first step is to take a bite-sized chunk, learn from it, recover from it, and then face the next one. As Eleanor Roosevelt once said, "You gain strength, courage, and confidence when you really stop to look fear in the face".

You must do the thing you cannot do. It could be as simple as saying "No" to your boss. Fear of losing your job may make you reluctant to act, and as a result you're treated in a way that doesn't align with your values. As Dorothy Thompson wrote, "Only when we are no longer afraid do we begin to live".

I kind of agree with what she says.

I think we need to accept that fear is part of the process. We need to feel it, see it, and then quickly move on before it drags us back to habitual patterns of fear. Once you build your courage around fear, you'll slowly 'power up' your life as the boundaries that restricted you begin to crumble.

Fear is a powerful emotion and great motivator. On Saturday afternoons, several Australian Champions in various martial arts would attend an open sparring session.

It was very popular, with more than 30 black belts taking part in some sessions. Top fighters used this session to prepare for major competitions, including:

- Adam Watt (4 times world kickboxing champion)
- Colin Handley (9 times Australian heavyweight Taekwondo Champion)
- Tom Lilovac (Australian Karate Champion).

I designed my entire training program around surviving the Saturday session. It had so many different martial arts, and all under the one roof. But unless you prepared you didn't last long.

My workout would start on the Thursday as I felt the fear start to rise. The argument over whether or not to go would rage inside my head until I put on the gloves and started sparring.

It helped my overcome my fear. It also helped me lay the groundwork (and create a formula) for moving beyond my comfort zone in other areas of my life.

Getting so many great fighters together from so many styles was a celebration of what was possible. I don't think it's been done or seen since.

See it, fear it, and do it.

When I was living in Japan, the fear often presented itself as self-talk at around lunchtime on training day. I'd hear my inner voice tell me, "It's raining. Why don't you forget about training for tonight?"

I was always scared when training at the Daito Ryu Headquarters in Tokyo. The training was always intense and painful. Kondo Sensei was an angry and intense man, and he'd unleash a tirade of abuse if you messed up the etiquette of the dojo in any way.

I found it really difficult, as I went from being an Aussie boy to what felt like being an attendant in the Japanese royal household.

In Kondo Sensei's dojo I was immediately expected to understand the intricacies of what that entailed. It was tough, and my only saving grace was the fact he yelled at me in Japanese, which I didn't understand a word of.

But as I learned Japanese it really started to sting. I remember all the students and teachers being at a restaurant for a birthday celebration. Sensei was sitting down, and I stood beside him and started talking to him. He suddenly exploded in an unforgettable tirade of Japanese profanities. Apparently it was considered rude to stand and talk to sensei while he was sitting. I had no idea.

At times I felt like a schoolboy who was afraid of the headmaster.

The fear ramped up on the 20-minute walk from the station to the dojo. It would come in waves, and I was often tempted to turn around and go home. But I just felt it, and recognised it was just a thought and had no power over me. And I kept putting one foot in front of the other until I reached the dojo.

When I arrived, I'd be welcomed by the unmistakeable smell of the dojo and the 'boom, boom' of people hitting the floor from break falling.

I kept moving forward no matter what my mind was telling me. The fear was there, but it had absolutely no grip on me. It worked for a full year. I missed only one or two classes the entire time I was in Japan. My brother Nip (John) and I even trained at the dojo on Christmas Day.

Fear will always be there. And it will justify itself in any number of ways. Sometimes fear is good, and protects you from harm. But it can also prevent you from living a vital and fulfilling life. As one of my teachers used to say, "See it, feel it, observe it, then work back and try to find the cause. When you have that, work back again. And again."

It's always good to find out what's *really* causing the fear.

Don't get pushed around
When someone pushes you, move to the side and let them pass. This takes strength of mind, as your previous reaction may have been to resist, make a point or give your opinion. Just try to be still and quiet every now and then and see what happens.

The space between others
Become aware of the space between you and others. Awareness of that space means you can control it. Once you build that awareness, you quickly become aware of how you move in other people's space. Next time you feel a desperate need to get your stuff done, stop and make sure you aren't moving into other people's space.

"What's in it for me?"
Acknowledge other people's support and care by showing gratitude. Generosity of spirit strengthens your ability to forgive, and opens your heart to receive. "What's in it for me?" has no place here.

Keep your own counsel
Own your thoughts, actions, plans and dreams. Only you know how much they mean to you. If you're constantly swayed by the crowd, surprise yourself and everyone else by believing your own uniqueness is special and worthy. This is how you develop leadership skills.

Accept change
When you're fighting you must adapt and move very quickly. The moment you get set in your ways you get hit. It's a great metaphor for living. If you become adamant that your reality will never change, you'll face incredible suffering when it does.

Be fluid, supple, and friendly with life. And promise yourself that from this moment on you'll never be less than friendly towards yourself.

Just watch thoughts as you would watch clouds passing by in the sky. There is nothing personal about your thoughts. They are just phenomena passing through awareness.

> "Meditation is not a technique to master; it is the highest form of prayer, a naked act of love and effortless surrender into the silent abyss beyond all knowing."
>
> – Adyashanti, *The way of liberation*

CONNECT

Have you seen the movie *Into the wild*? It's a true story about a man who spends his entire life running from people and wanting to be alone. He ends up isolating himself in an old caravan in the Alaskan wilderness. At the end of the story, trapped by the winter and dying from lack of food, he writes "We are not meant to be alone" in his journal. I'm sure we've all wanted to be alone and have time to ourselves at some point. And the idea of solitude can be appealing at first. But while most people can choose to isolate themselves from everyone else, others don't have that option. They're alone simply because of how their life unfolded.

Despite us having so many ways to connect with each other, loneliness and isolation have become more and more common. Most of us yearn for connection, for love, and to be part of a larger family, club, organisation or regular social interaction. But a lot of people are afraid to take ownership of the self-serving ways that are keeping them separated and alone.

In today's society, most of us don't know our neighbours and feel threatened by anyone who smiles at us. But no matter how we feel about ourselves and other people, it's natural (and very human) to want to love and be loved. So even if you're happy being alone, a small part of you still yearns for some sort of connection.

There are many limitations that can stop us from making and

maintaining these connections. These limitations start with how we think and feel about ourselves. Before we can connect with other people, we need to connect with ourselves.

There are plenty of books out there on how to change your life by changing your thoughts. *The Happiness Trap* by Russ Harris and *Change your thinking* by Sarah Edelman are two of my favourites.

In his great book *The essential laws of fearless living*, Guy Finley clearly points out one of life's and humankind's biggest afflictions: "What's in it for me?" and that every interaction, no matter how pure and honest it seems, is governed by what we'll get out of it.

Guy offers the following as a great way to start improving how we relate.

1. What we would have from others or have them be towards us, we must provide or be ourselves.
2. Before we ask for someone's attention, let us first lend that person our own.
3. Before we look to him for an act of consideration, let us offer one for ourselves.
4. If we wish kindness, let it begin with our own. Otherwise all we give are unconscious demands, followed by judgement and disappointment.

Simple ways to connect

When I was in hospital, the therapy included the importance of connecting with people. Here's what I've been using to create and maintain important connections for the past 20 years.

Start with a smile to make a connection. A smile enlivens your own face, and sends a clear message to others that you care. Smiling also dissipates anxiety, frustration and anger. And who doesn't like a smiling, happy face? Everyone profits from a smile.

Talk to people. Say "Hello," and ask them how their day is going. You'll be surprised at what comes back. Your only motive is to connect.

Stop and listen. When someone is talking to you, actively and consciously listen. Don't be in a hurry, and ignore the self-talk that's going on. Look them in the eye. No-one likes talking to some one who is preoccupied and looking over their shoulder.

Keep a social log. Make a list of your friends and family, and keep a log of when you last contacted them, and how and when you last met. Try and contact them at least once a month.

Schedule regular coffee/lunches with friends and family. Don't let the old "I don't have time. I'm too busy" way of thinking fool you.

You can connect with people in any number of ways. Fear may stop you from extending, but don't let it stop you from doing something you really want to do.

Try good old-fashioned letters or postcards to connect. You could also try phone calls, texts, emails, blogs, or even social media platforms such as Facebook and Twitter. These days we're spoiled for choice, and so there's really no excuse.

Reach out, and don't worry about rejection. You'll never be judged for being friendly and opening your heart. Even if people don't accept or welcome you, you'll feel better and more connected. Just because someone doesn't get back to you doesn't mean they don't want to be your friend. They may feel disconnected, and your message could mean a lot to them.

We're all on this journey together. And we all have a one-way ticket home. Why not see if we can be happy by improving the quality of people's lives around us? Reaching out across the void of negativity and depression, and smiling, helping and offering unconditional service.

MONEY

This may seem like a strange topic for this book, especially seeing as people generally like to keep their financial situation private. But I think I can help, and so I've decided to talk about it.

Money isn't a dirty word. But it can create a lot of pain and suffering.

Attending martial arts and working towards your black belt takes time and discipline. Each class you attend is one step closer to your eventual goal. There are no shortcuts.

Saving money and paying off loans are similar. Saving for the long term takes discipline and commitment, as does paying off a loan.

Here are some simple rules I use that are often overlooked.

More isn't always better

I often wondered what the magical formula was for making money. I tried all kinds of short cuts. But after making it and losing it not once but twice, I think I finally get it. I now believe that the more you make and try to hold onto, the more you lose. And the more you're attached to it when you lose it, the more you suffer.

This might sound a little severe. We all need money to live, and when we don't have it our sense of security is understandably diminished. (Especially now that the cost of living is higher than ever.) The competition for rental properties (not to mention properties for sale) is fuelled by our ever-increasing population.

We demand higher wages so we can afford mortgage repayments. And because we're always being told that more is better, consumer debt is even higher.

So how on earth do you get ahead? Here are some simple strategies I've used over the years that have helped me keep my head above water. And I hope they help you too.

Love what you do

Why is a martial arts teacher writing about money? Because part of my personal journey has been managing my desire for security while earning a living educating people about personal growth.

For years I struggled with the misguided notion that because I was charging to teach martial arts I was selling out on the art. But realising my income was allowing me to empower more people was a real lightbulb moment. You'll spend a large proportion of your life working, so make sure you love it. Doing what you love (to the point where you're living, breathing and oozing passion) is a great first step towards taking control of your finances. Because when you love what you do, you don't need any time off.

Clear debt

There's no point in saving or getting low interest rates if you don't pay off your high-interest credit card first – specially seeing as most people pay credit with post-tax dollars. It's negative economics. I use my credit card all the time, especially as it accrues frequent flyer points. But if you pay it off by the monthly payment due date, it's interest free.

Take control

Running your own business isn't for everyone. But being in control of your own destiny can give you is great sense of freedom and accomplishment. The money you earn is directly proportional to the effort you put in. There are no shortcuts, but if you have a good work ethic the rewards can be outstanding.

However, this doesn't mean you need to leave your full-time job.

Not yet, anyway. There are great part-time business opportunities where most of the upfront cost is effort and the desire to succeed. And you get to pay legitimate business expenses with pre-tax dollars. (Your accountant can help you with this.)

Turn a hobby into a business

I've run several businesses that were good rather than great. I hated the work, but persisted because I was good at it. These included working as:

- a gardener
- a doorman
- a plumber
- a tradesman for an agency
- a salesperson for a water filtration installation business.

In each case I taught martial arts at the same time. But I had trouble accepting it was okay to charge for it, and so I preferred to call it a hobby.

Realising your worth

I had an idea. I wanted to apply the customer service I learned in the service industry to martial arts. I also wanted to:

- rehash the programs to make the classes fun but challenging for all ages and fitness levels
- make obtaining a black belt an achievable goal for both men and women.

It meant a complete name and brand change. But the fact I was unemployed meant I had nothing to lose. (I'd already lost it all twice.)

So I changed the name from Fightclub to Northstar, and gave my full attention to running a successful martial arts school. And while empowering others through martial arts I:

- recovered financially from a divorce
- saved for a deposit
- bought a house
- paid off the mortgage in four years.

I now teach martial arts online. I also do a lot of writing, and happily share my knowledge.

I've followed these steps to become debt-free and own my home. Owning your own house is the first step towards financial freedom. I'm obviously not an investment expert, and to be fully self-sufficient you need to think about superannuation and other investments. But here are some pointers you might find helpful.

- Live within your means.
- Spend less than you earn.
- Pay yourself first.
- Create a budget.
- Clear your credit card debt every month.
- Save for the long term.
- Have a mortgage offset account.
- Work hard.
- Enjoy your work.

Living a disciplined life

A warrior must live a disciplined life. Unless you live a disciplined life, it's too easy to get involved with stuff. People use their car horn as a weapon because you're not moving as fast as they want you to.

When we had the hair-trigger threat of lockdown between 2020 and 2023, people understandably became very wound up. It was a time to show what you were really made of. The residual effects of COVID-19 still seem to be festering, and the care factor seems to be low. It's all just stuff.

You can tell your discipline training is working when you're no longer getting hooked into the drama. You don't feel the need to react, and can offset the stress of doing so. It's not because you're 'turning the other cheek', or don't have an opinion to offer. You're simply choosing which battles to take on.

I live a disciplined life. But I didn't achieve that discipline overnight.

With so many temptations out there these days, you can easily get caught up in petty rumours and negative talk about insignificant things. So when you *do* talk or give your opinion, do so as an act of kindness.

Warriors have no time for duplicity, gambling, drinking or 'chasing skirt'. So many so-called martial arts and spiritual leaders have ruined their lives by declaring they are an awakened master to followers only to be accused of sexual misconduct and retire early in shame.

One of my secrets of success is to keep showing up even when you don't feel like it. Everything we do will seem boring at times. But if we keep giving up every time it does, we'll never achieve anything. Whether it's your martial arts, your hobbies, or your relationships, just keep showing up. It will bring out a strength that you'll start to understand and use in the rest of your life.

STRIPPING OUT MY BATHROOM

THE NEW BATH IS IN AND MOST OF THE TILING IS DONE

PUTTING IN NEW PIPE WORK FOR MY NEW BATHROOM

INSTALLING THE TOILET IN MY NEW BATHROOM

BEING THROWN 100 TIMES

FIGHTING BLAIR PHILLIPS. ONE TOUGH GUY

SITTING IN SEIZA IN THE DOJO

WARRIOR TIPS

1. **Develop a sincere curiosity.** Replace the urge to judge or criticise with saying, "That's curious".
2. **Replace negative thoughts with thoughts of beauty.** For example, when I'm sitting in traffic I remind myself of the beauty around the great city I live in.
3. **Bathe in the present moment, and give each task your full attention.** Just try it.
4. **Train even when you don't feel like it. Your body and your mind will both thank you for it.**
5. **Develop your mindfulness.** Breath in, breath out. Know that you're breathing in and out.
6. **Get educated.** Start at least one course you've been meaning to take. There are so many courses you can do online. (The Duolingo app is great for learning languages.)
7. **Let go.** Pushing and rushing only attracts negativity. Releasing and 'being' taps into the universal flow. You need to give up to gain.
8. **Remember that this too shall pass.** Every situation – good or bad – will pass. Recognising this universal law enables nonattachment and suffering. (We mourn the most when we lose something.)
9. **Give more than you get.** As Gandhi says, "The fragrance remains in the hand that gives the rose". Give, and keep giving. Don't do it for a reason, and don't expect anything in return.

Try these for a day and see how you feel.

Brain surgery

If you've seen any of my video tapes or interviews pre-October 2020, you may have noticed that I couldn't keep my head still. It just rotated up and down, and around and around.

This is known as cervical dyskinesia.

Dyskinesia is a nasty side-effect of the dopamine replacement therapy I take in pill form five times a day. It can affect any part of the body. It's just bad luck I also have the cervical component that causes the head to rotate.

My specialist started getting concerned about the wear and tear on my cervical spine. It was becoming more of a problem than the Parkinson's itself. He recommended looking into Deep Brain Stimulation therapy.

At this point I was up for anything, and DBS was definitely an option. It was a little early for me to consider it as an option, but I was weighing it against my spine wearing out and the implications around that. So I agreed to all the pre-investigation checks to see whether I'd be a good candidate.

For the next few weeks I participated in a range of physical, neurological and psychological tests. And in the end I was deemed a good candidate. I asked for a number of 'second opinions', and was satisfied the team I'd chosen would do a good job. But who knows? This brain surgery came with a hefty price tag. But what price can you put on your health?

I'd spoken to others who'd had DBS, and with the dyskinesia getting worse it became obvious that something needed to be done. DBS was the best course of action, we set a date for the surgery.

How did I feel about having two 150mm probes being put deep into my brain while I was still awake?

Scared. Very scared.

Nothing anyone said prepared me for the surgery, and it turned out to be far worse than anyone cared to say. I was scared about the entire ordeal. But while I could have easily talked myself out of it, the reasons for having the surgery were too compelling.

So I focused on the good, and shut down thoughts like *One slip and I'm done for*. At times I felt an overwhelming dread and almost panicked. But I kept breathing, and remembering about the rope and the snake. I just kept moving forward.

The operation started, and they gave me a light sedative. I needed to be awake for the first three hours of the operation so I could help them place the probes correctly. The two surgeons and the neurologist secured my head firmly in a brace. This was incredibly difficult, as my head had been moving constantly for the past two years.

Then they started peeling back my scalp. Thanks to the local injections I didn't feel any pain. But I was acutely aware of having my hair pulled back.

And then came the drilling.

I can still remember the surgeon telling me I had a thick skull. It seemed like an eternity of drilling, and the pressure on my head was intense. It felt like the drill would break through my skull at any second. Death would be quick.

Once they'd finished drilling, they needed to set the parameters of the electrical probes. I needed to be awake so I could give them feedback. I also needed to keep my eyes open to create an electric pulse. But they'd also given me a couple of injections to relax my eyelids. So there I was with head in a brace, two holes in my head, two probes deep in my brain, and a neurologist screaming at me to keep my eyes open despite being given injections for me to close them.

Then at last I felt myself slip into oblivion.

The anaesthetist put me under so they could tidy up my skull, put the electric neurostimulator under the skin on my chest, and run wires up my neck to join the probes in my brain. By the end I was well connected, and expecting to light up like a Christmas tree.

After six hours I was done. I woke up in the intensive care ward, and the stimulator was turned on.

That was in October 2020, and since then the tremor, stiffness and dyskinesia have all disappeared completely.

One thing I realised is how difficult it had been to wipe my bottom. My torso had been so rigid that it was hard to turn. But after the operation I could turn with ease and wipe my backside properly again – a small luxury.

Many people with Parkinson's talk about being robbed. Yes, it's an insidious disease that presents itself every morning to pick up where it left off the night before.

It's been two years since I had the operation. I still don't have any tremor, stiffness or rigidity. But I still take my medication, because the other symptoms of Parkinson's (the ones you don't hear about) are slowly ramping up.

I have REM sleep disorder, which is where you act out your dreams (much to the chagrin of your partner). Unfortunately my dreams are usually violent, and I find myself kicking and punching 2-3 imaginary opponents. Having trained in martial arts for more than 40 years, I can feel the power of the moves in my sleep.

So Liz and I prepare the bedroom every night. We've changed our bed so it's closer to the ground. We put pillows on the floor, and pillows between us. Liz is a light sleeper, and she'll gently wake me up if I start getting agitated. But I go to sleep never knowing how the night will develop. Sometimes I wake up lying at the bottom of the bed, with no idea how I got there.

Some days I'm very tired, and need to really motivate myself to move. But I do. I just keep moving. At 7am I take my first round of pills and then ease into my chi gong, a short routine to get started. Liz gets me a turmeric tea and a glass of water with apple cider vinegar to reduce the inflammation in my body. I then run through 10 martial arts kicking and punching routines. They're great for balance and memory, and I do them as fast as I can.

In 2018 I had an ankle fusion. My ankle has caused me more grief than Parkinson's ever has.

Stress can have a very negative effect on my day. I try to keep it to a minimum, as it really affects my ability to concentrate.

The effects of Sifrol

As I mentioned earlier, I supplement the effects of the deep brain stimulation with Parkinson's medication that address the non-motor symptoms of the disease. There's currently nothing that can stop the disease. All we have is medication to reduce the symptoms. They're very effective, but the disease just keeps getting worse. Fund raisers such as Michael J Fox and Clyde Campbell from the Shake it Up Australia Foundation have made incredible inroads to stopping this disease, and even better, finding a cure. One of the medications I take is Sifrol, which comes from the group of pills called dopamine agonists. After more than two years of medication, my Neurologist has prescribed a very low dose of Sifrol. The funny thing is one of its possible side-effects is a form of obsessive, compulsive behaviour. A high dose can lead to excessive spending, gambling or hypersexuality. Knowing my history, this would be dangerous for me. I felt myself getting worked up and anxiety is also one of the side effects as well as hallucinations. Liz mentioned to me that I was changing without me realising it. So I stopped the Sifrol, and will talk to Dr Rowe, my specialist next time I see him.

Living day-to-day with Parkinson's

One thing that's always resonated with me is what Clyde Campbell, founder of the Shake it Up Australia Foundation, said to me when I was first diagnosed with Parkinson's disease. He said, "It's important to understand that this is the start of the journey, and that you can work on how you function with Parkinson's to the very best of your ability. It's not the beginning of the end".

I often reflect on his words as I try to find a sweet spot between sleep, exercise, diet, medication, the side-effects of the meds and the advice of my wellness team. Unfortunately, just when you think you've nailed it because you've had a good day, the next day is terrible and you have no idea why. You do everything according to schedule, and then whammo, the meds suddenly aren't working anymore.

It's as if I'm covered with a thick wet blanket. All I can do is shuffle and shake between commitments, and keep believing it will all be better soon. I could take more medication, but that would increase the horrible side-effects of dyskinesia – a frustratingly benign involuntary movement of my head, hand and foot. So between the Parkinson's tremor and the dyskinesia, it's little wonder I stay close to home.

I was once strong and fast. I could get in, score multiple shots on my opponent and move back out of range in a blink of an eye, all without a hand being laid on me. It's something I took for granted, thinking I'd always be that fast.

And I was an even faster talker. I used to say "The whole world's on 'go slow' drugs" because I moved quickly no matter what I was doing.

Fast forward 30 years, and that life seems like someone else's. But being diagnosed with a chronic and progressive neurological illness at 54 did speed up one thing. It quickly put how I run my life (once I accepted it was really happening) into perspective. These days I need to adjust and reinvent myself every minute rather than every day.

I try to find the humour in it all and laugh at myself. I post as many funny photos of myself on social media as possible. It's all very human, because I'm not Superman anymore.

I work out as much as I can. Walking is a treat, and I do as much yoga and Pilates as my body allows. I meditate every morning. Sitting with no movement at all is a gift. My body gives me a reprieve in the mornings, as if it's forgotten I have PD. So I use the time for deep reflection, savouring every second.

I'm planning on doing a 10-day silent meditation retreat soon. Hopefully my body will let me, but life must go on regardless.

Most afternoons I head into my private dojo, turn up the music, and punch and kick the bags and ride the stationary bike. It feels great doing this. I feel alive, and a little dangerous. I'm flying, and no-one can stop me.

There is no doubt that Parkinson's effects my daily routine.

But I remember Clyde Campbell saying to me, teaching with Parkinson's will be an entirely new experience for me, that will really test my warrior spirit. I won't give in.

Having Parkinson's disease, I've seen some incredible examples of warriorship – people facing immense adversity but still maintaining an incredible attitude towards it.

The thing about Parkinson's is it changes from day to day. So I have rituals that give me the best shot at having a productive day. It all starts with having a good night's sleep and waking up refreshed. The next important point is not to load up my day. Stress knocks my socks off. I'm careful about what, when and how much I eat. I try to exercise every day. I also do callisthenics and lift weights.

People often comment on how well and strong I look. But that's on a good day. On a not-so-good day my jaw chatters uncontrollably, I'm exhausted by 9am, and I struggle to motivate myself in any way. But I know I need to, and so I heave myself up and try to do something, anything. My typing is difficult, my speech is hard to understand, and you'll never get me on the phone.

The point of the medication is to have a smooth transition between pill times. So you need to keep adjusting it until there are no 'off' times. But you can't just keep increasing it, as the side-effects are terrible.

I just need to make it through the day, because I'm sure the next one will be better.

But I teach no matter how I'm feeling. Nothing gets in the way of that. I'll do whatever it takes to pass on the Northstar Ju Jitsu System. I'm blessed that I can still move my arms and legs and show the techniques. And I'm lucky that I don't fall apart and suffer from depression. I keep good people around me –people who nourish my soul.

One thing I've found is that Parkinson's doesn't like new experiences and hates exercise. Whenever I experience a holiday, a new restaurant or anything else that's new, Parkinson's remains quiet. It also behaves when I exercise, and I don't feel it. So I relish these times.

Will I die from Parkinson's? I don't think so. But the final stages of Parkinson's aren't pretty. As I was developing the first symptoms of Parkinson's, I watched my mother slowly disappear when her Parkinson's took her over. It was terrible to watch. I try not to recall or think about her passing. So many things that can take you. But I'm not afraid of dying so much as I am afraid of not living.

Will there be a cure? Good question. There are so many research pathways, and there's more hope now than ever before. But I try not to get excited. I just live my life knowing what I know right now. I make every day a good day regardless of how I'm feeling. If there is a treatment, great. But if there isn't then I'll make the most out of what I have.

And that's what true warriorhood is all about.

I'm now going to leave you with the introduction to my next book. I hope you enjoy it.

Introduction of the next book I am working on

When I was 18 I had quite an unnerving experience. Some would even call it 'spiritual'.

I'd been interested in meditation for a long time. At the time there weren't any real books on how to meditate, so I started out with *Jonathan Livingston Seagull* and Shirley MacLaine's books.

I learned to meditate at the *Friends of the Western Buddhist Society*. It was a wonderful time, and it really opened my mind. All the enquiry, introspection and meditation opened me up to a new way of living.

But I was too naïve to follow it up. I got swallowed by the ego, and it completely blocked that time of my life. I was catapulted into achieving, and wasn't ready for the spiritual learning. If only I'd the strength to stand up to my ego and follow the path staring me in the face. It took 40-plus years and a world of pain for me to return to the spiritual path.

What was so special about this time? I've always felt a connection with something else. I don't know what it is, and it's hard to put it into words. (This is the first time I've ever tried to explain it.) But if I had say what that 'something' was, I'd say another dimension. I know that sounds corny, but it's the way for me to explain it.

The first time I felt something was around 7 years old. I was awake early, and because I was afraid of the dark I got into the bed with my mother and pulled the sheets and blankets over my head. I soon became aware of someone (or something) coming into the room and standing beside the bed. But when I pulled bed sheets back the room was empty.

These weren't just the imaginings of a young boy. There was something or someone there. I was sure I wasn't alone, and I'll never forget the feeling.

Fast-forward to when I was 18. It was midnight on a Friday, and I'd just dropped my girlfriend back home (a 15-minute drive from my place). The road wasn't dark as it was illuminated by the streetlights. There was a fine mist and it was damp, but the weather was good.

Suddenly, what I can only describe as the upper bodies of two ghouls appeared on the road directly in front of me. I slammed on the brakes, but I drove right through them and their torsos flashed through the car.

And that was it, or so I thought.

The following night, driving down the street after dropping my girlfriend home, I ended up at the same spot I'd had my weird experience the night before.

I turned into the main street, and immediately noticed there weren't any other cars around. Suddenly the entire street in front of me and a huge tree that overhung the road were completely illuminated by an intense light. I slowed down from 60 to 40, and my front tyre suddenly burst. I knew something evil would happen to me if I pulled over to fix it, and so I drove my car all the way home. (It completely ruined the tyre and the wheel.)

This experience, and what happened the night before, really unnerved me. I had no reference point to understand what had happened. So I thought the best plan of action was to forget about it. And so it just sat there in the back room of my mind.

When I was in my early twenties I was living in a share house in Glebe and working as a plumber. Nothing special, just making do. At this point I'd been doing a lot of meditation, but hadn't had any experiences I'd consider 'spiritual'. So I don't think meditation had any influence on what I'm about to tell you.

I was lying downstairs on the floor. I wasn't asleep, just relaxed. Suddenly I was in another place. I knew it wasn't a dream because I was fully awake. I looked down the length of my body and saw

I was wearing armour, including steel-pointed armoured boots. I was tall, and had shoulder-length dark hair and a short beard.

I was in a large tent with the flap open. I smelled cut grass, and the ambience was fresh.

I knew what this ancient warrior was thinking. He was going to war that day, and didn't think he'd be coming back. Since I was a boy I've had pain in the armpit of my left arm. I'd even been to several doctors to get it checked. But after this vision the pain disappeared. I took a spear in my armpit and died in battle.

This experience happened very quickly, and for an instant the mind was quiet, which allowing me to experience it in detail. But as soon as my ego/mind went *Whoa. What's happening?* the vision dissolved and I was back in the room, wondering what had just happened.

I've tried to repeat the experience, but nothing has worked. And so I believe I had a spontaneous past-life regression. *(more to come)*

ACKNOWLEDGEMENTS

So many people have been instrumental to my healing and growth as a person. And they've all been a great inspiration for this book.

I mentioned Daryl Baulkham as one. He put his arm around me when I really needed it and kept me moving. The late John Cooper, who taught me so much about life, would often say I'm too uptight and driven, and remind me of the importance of living now. My family. My older brother Rob, who found himself homeless at 60. You truly are an inspiration, bro. I've watched you struggle, and you just keep moving forward.

Thank you to my older sister Melanie and her husband Martin for forgiving me and being so gracious about it. Belinda, I hope we meet again soon. John, who has kept the nickname Nip from the time he was a boy. He shared many of the tough times with me, and is so much stronger and resilient than me. My son Tom. Love you son. My nieces and nephews – Will, Ellen, Hunter, Jasper and Jay. I've really enjoyed getting to know you. I would also like to acknowledge my step mother Gayle for your unconditional support, and my sister Georgina.

Liz, your calm, quiet love gives me strength to keep going when the times are tough. I love our life together.

And finally to all the unsung warriors I have the honour of calling my friends; John Saw, my Chi Gong Master and Alison Anderson, my Tai Chi Master. Darren Higgs from Quantum Martial Arts, Robin Dosoruth from Arrow

Martial Arts, Stephen Renton from Weststar Martial Arts. You guys keep the Northstar Ju Jitsu flame burning.

You've all motivated me to be so much more than I thought I could ever be. You remain my unconditional friends, and I know we'll pick up our friendship exactly where we left off.

ABOUT ME

I live in Sydney's Inner West with Liz my wife. I do a lot of writing between meditation and enquiry. We are quite close to the water and parks.

I love a good belly laugh. I've made a Facebook account with the funniest videos I come across. Most of them are quite ridiculous, but they appeal to my sense of humour. I try to have a good laugh every morning.

I've become a writer. I have had no formal education in writing, but there was a glimmer of talent when I did creative writing at school. It was a talent I never investigated. Whenever I think about missed opportunities, this is what I think about.

I was a Wise Man in the Christmas pageant at my first school. I was 5 years old, and I remember wearing the Bedouin clothing. It was all very serious, and I really enjoyed my first foray into acting. I didn't get another chance until I was in Year 5, age 11, when played the main part in The Flying Pieman school stage production. I really enjoyed that too. Oh, well. I've often wondered what kind of actor I would have been. Did anyone else see my potential?

I love to travel and try new hotels and restaurants. But the years flying as a flight attendant really spoiled me. From the hotel on Nobs Hill in San Francisco to a hotel on the Danube River in Germany, it was just one hotel to the next with a handful of money. No such glamour these days.

I sing and dance most mornings. I belt out songs I know, and my dancing is atrocious. But I don't care who's watching or listening. I'm having a great time.

I grab Liz and we do our tango, a skill I picked up years ago. I love it, and it is like riding a bike – you never forget the moves. Thank you, Pedro, for your never-ending patience.

I usually read 3-5 books at a time. I listen to Audible and watch cooking shows on YouTube, hunting for simple and tasty meals to eat. I love to bake, and Tom loves it too, especially my banana cake. I often tempt him over with a freshly baked banana cake.

Meditation is one of my pillars. I watch the mind for thinking that doesn't empower me, even if only for 10 minutes a day.

I love my coffee, and will spend time watching the water and the birds at Hen and Chicken Bay.

Oh, and I have Parkinson's and I am a 'warrior' with everything that encompasses.

I have an online learning portal called The Mastery Academy *(northstarmartialarts.com.au)* that covers pretty much everything from martial arts to meditation. The online Mastery Academy is where I now teach and is the culmination of my 40 years of training and research. I also teach The Warrior Upgrade online.

If you have any questions you can email me at
admin@northstarmartialarts.com.au

Or send a message via:
Instagram/northstarjujitsu
Facebook.com/northstarjujitsu
www.northstarmartialarts.com.au

I also have a personal website:
www.andydickinson.com.au

APPENDIX

The following qualities are followed to Warrior Upgrade your life. If you choose to follow a warrior path, then his book will give you my take on what it means to follow that path. It will require your commitment to yourself and your desire to get the most out of your life. Follow this way and you will be catapulted to where you want to be. Not held back by fear or anxiety. You choose to live a good life, a warrior life. It worked for me.

1. **The Way**
2. **Discipline**
3. **Honesty**
4. **Spirit**
5. **Determination**
6. **Respect**
7. **Action**
8. **Now**
9. **Recycle**
10. **Change**
11. **Be on time**
12. **Show your neck**
13. **Stress**
14. **Make it count**
15. **Take massive action**
16. **Balance**
17. **Space**
18. **Fear**
19. **Connect**
20. **Money**

www.ingramcontent.com/pod-product-compliance
Lightning Source LLC
Chambersburg PA
CBHW070307010526
44107CB00056B/2522